# Homeowner's Complete Guide
# to the Chainsaw

# Homeowner's Complete Guide to the Chainsaw

by Brian J. Ruth & Jen W. Ruth

A **chainsaw pro** shows you how to *safely* and *confidently* handle everything from **trimming** branches and **felling** trees to **splitting** and **stacking** wood.

FOX CHAPEL
PUBLISHING

## IMPORTANT NOTICE TO READERS!

Because working with chainsaws, sharp tools, trees and brush, and other materials shown in this book inherently includes the risk of injury and damage, this book cannot guarantee that following procedures in this book will be safe for everyone. For this reason, this book is sold without warranties or guarantees of any kind, expressed or implied, and the publisher and the authors disclaim liability for any injuries, losses, or damages caused in any way by the content of this book or the reader's use of the tools needed to complete the projects presented here. The publisher and the authors urge all chainsaw operators to thoroughly review each project and procedures and to understand the use of all tools before beginning any project or procedure.

© 2009 by Fox Chapel Publishing Company, Inc.
*Homeowner's Complete Guide to the Chainsaw* is an original work, first published in 2009 by Fox Chapel Publishing Company, Inc.

Photos by Scott Kriner, John Kelsey, Daniel Clarke, and Troy Thorne.

Drawings courtesy Skills Institute Press.

The safety information in this book was reviewed by Dale J. Cagwin, P.E.

ISBN 978-1-56523-356-0

Library of Congress Cataloging-in-Publication Data

Ruth, Brian J.

Homeowner's complete guide to the chainsaw : a chainsaw pro shows you how to safely and confidently handle everything from trimming branches and felling trees to splitting and stacking wood / by Brian J. Ruth and Jen W. Ruth.

    p. cm.

ISBN: 978-1-56523-356-0

1. Chain saws--Handbooks, manuals, etc. 2. Chainsaws--Maintenance and repair. 3. Trees, Care of. 4. Trees--Pruning. I. Ruth, Jen W. II. Title.

TJ1233.R88 2009
621.9'34--dc22                          2009015635

To learn more about the other great books from Fox Chapel Publishing, or to find a retailer near you, call toll free 800-457-9112 or visit us at *www.FoxChapelPublishing.com*.

**Note to Authors:** We are always looking for talented authors to write new books in our area of woodworking, design, and related crafts. Please send a brief letter describing your idea to Acquisition Editor, 1970 Broad Street, East Petersburg, PA 17520.

Printed in China
First printing: July 2009

# Introduction

What if you didn't grow up with a chainsaw, or don't have a friend to teach you, what do you do then?

That is what this book is all about. It is meant to introduce you to the chainsaw. We'll spell out the differences among the various saws so you can choose the one that is right for you. We'll help you understand how it works and what happens when its chain contacts what you're cutting. We will walk you through various projects and the methods of using the saw to complete those projects. We will show you essential safety gear, and how to maintain your saw. Most of all, we'll show you safe methods of working so that if you choose to run a chainsaw you can do it safely and effectively.

I've been running a chainsaw for so long I hardly remember how I learned. I remember standing by the saw buck as my father and grandfather placed the logs up on it for me to cut. I think I was about thirteen the first time. My grandfather bought that saw from a preacher. My father gave it to me as a keepsake and we still have that saw. It's an old Mall electric with a rear pistol grip and a short front handle grip. It was very heavy, and the wiser of the group were more than happy to let me have my fun and tire myself out by running the saw—which I did, every chance I got. I would relish the thought of having to cut more firewood.

In high school I got a job with a small tree service. My job was to feed the chipper and cut up anything that was downed by one of the climbers. It was a dream job: good pay, outdoors, and most important, I got to run a chainsaw. It didn't take long until I

This antique monster saw weighs a ton and you have to pivot the engine in its housing to keep the carburetor upright, or else it floods and stalls. This wasn't my first saw, but it sure does illustrate how far we've come from the professional-only saws of yesterday to homeowner-friendly saws today.

was asking if I could do some climbing. My workmate Joe was an excellent climber. He instructed me on notches and roping down limbs and staying alive running a chainsaw a hundred feet up a tree.

I did tree work all through my college years and I consider that time as my chainsaw survival training. By the time I started chainsaw carving I had a great feel for the bite of a chainsaw and it was only the art aspect that I had to learn. I have been lucky in more ways than one. I practically grew up with a chainsaw, I had the world's best teachers, and in all the years of working with the world's most dangerous power tool, I haven't needed more than a band aid.

—Brian Ruth, Lehighton, PA, May 2009

# Contents

Bucking your own firewood becomes easy and safe when you choose a saw with an anti-kickback nose guard, and take the time to build a construction-lumber sawbuck.

# This Book Will Teach You About:

**Safely operating a chainsaw
in your backyard**
Page 10

**Potential problems and real solutions**
Page 18

**Purchasing the chainsaw that
will best meet your needs**
Page 28

**Picking supplies and equipment you will
need to safely operate your chainsaw**
Page 43

**Safely starting your chainsaw**
Page 64

**Cutting Firewood (Bucking)**
Page 72

**Making and Using a Sawbuck**
Page 84

**Splitting and Stacking Firewood**
Page 92

**Trimming Overhead Branches**
Page 100

**Trimming a Hedge**
Page 104

**Felling a Small Tree**
Page 108

**Felling a Large Tree with Wedges**
Page 118

**Limbing a Downed Tree**
Page 126

**Felling and Limbing a Tree Near a House**
Page 134

**Cutting Down a Stump**
Page 148

**Milling Lumber From Logs**
Page 154

**When to Bring in a Professional**
Page 164

**Maintenance, Servicing, and Sharpening**
Page 168

# CHAPTER 1

# Read This Chapter!
## (Safety is Important)

**M**ost power tool owner's manuals, like most how-to books, start with a section about safety. The problem is, it's a boring list that many readers skip right over. They want to start using their new machine and do not want to waste time reading the same old safety rules.

The chainsaw, however, is not like other power tools. It is an extremely effective tree-cutting and branch-cutting machine. It works because it is an engine driving a sharp-toothed chain around a long, exposed guide bar. The fast-moving cutters can't be guarded, and consequently, the chainsaw is the most dangerous hand-held power tool in the world. Because of how the machine works, a chainsaw injury is liable to be a deep and ragged cut requiring many stitches and taking a long time to heal. You absolutely do not want to have a chainsaw accident.

That's why I must discuss safety right up front in this book, so you can avoid an accident while you learn to use your saw. (Please see reader advisory on page 4.)

Along with the saw itself, successful chainsaw operators must also purchase and use personal protective equipment. It's not optional and can't be postponed until later. Personal protective equipment includes a hard hat, a face shield and goggles for eye protection, hearing protection, leather work gloves, Kevlar-reinforced chaps for leg protection, and steel-toed boots. Yes, you do need all of it. No kidding around.

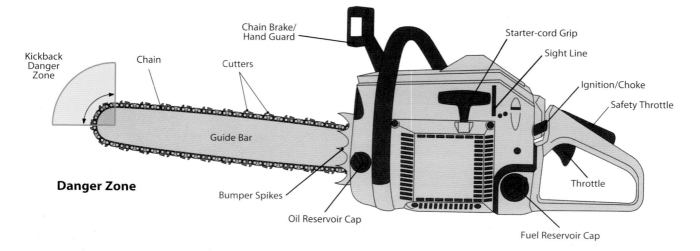

Kickback Danger Zone · Chain · Cutters · Chain Brake/Hand Guard · Starter-cord Grip · Sight Line · Ignition/Choke · Safety Throttle · Guide Bar · Throttle · **Danger Zone** · Bumper Spikes · Oil Reservoir Cap · Fuel Reservoir Cap

# The Risks

The risk of an accident or injury is always present, but actually having the mishap is entirely avoidable. It's entirely up to you. Your attitude is key to not ever having a serious chainsaw accident. You have to decide to take seriously this business of learning how to use your chainsaw safely and well. You must put safety uppermost. In this chapter, I'll tell you more about what that means.

With a new chainsaw in your hands, it's very tempting to jump right over the obligatory pages of safety rules and exhortations and to get right into the "Assembly" or "Operating Your New Tool" sections of the owner's manual.

Let me say right now that is not a good idea with a chainsaw. It's OK if you don't want to read the safety information first. Maybe you are itching to assemble your new tool, and read about how to operate it. OK good, but do not plug in the chainsaw (if it is electric) or put any fuel into it (if it is gas-powered) until you have gone back and completely read all of the safety information in the owner's manual. Here's why:

- **The chain** in a chainsaw can move up to 68 mph. That is incredibly fast and you are holding that speed in your hands.
- **At full speed,** more than 600 teeth will pass a given point per second. You cannot possibly react fast enough to get a hand, arm, leg, or your head out of the way.
- **Eighty-five percent** of chainsaw injuries come from contact with a moving chain.
- **There are more** than 100,000 chainsaw-related injuries every year in the United States. In 2007, the U.S. Product Safety

Commission estimated that more than 26,000 chainsaw injuries were treated in hospital emergency rooms.

- **The average number of stitches** from a chainsaw accident is 110.
- **A chainsaw** is one of the world's most dangerous handheld power tools—especially in the hands of a new user.
- **There are good reasons** why the chainsaw is a prop in many horror movies. Had enough? Me too.

Rather than giving you a long list of safety rules at this point, I'm going to discuss the problem more broadly, to help you understand the risks involved as well as your strategies for minimizing each risk.

## LEARNING SAFETY

If you are a new chainsaw user or even if you have used one a few times before, here is my recommendation for the best way to learn about chainsaw safety. First, read this book cover to cover to get an understanding of how a chainsaw works and how to use one safely. Then, read the owner's manual for your particular chainsaw, because it should make more sense after reading this book and will have additional information that will apply to your particular saw. Next, read the "Important Safety Rules" in your owner's manual, because by then you will understand why they are important. And finally, think about safety and ask about safety while you learn how to use your chainsaw. Make it a habit to put on your safety gear, and think about safety, every time you use the saw. Take personal responsibility for not hurting yourself or anyone else while you work. Make it a point of personal pride.

**Accident Location and Frequency**

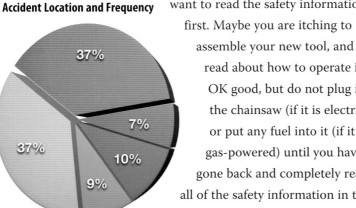

37%

7%

37%

10%

9%

- ● Head Area
- ● Hand Area
- ● Foot Area
- ● Upper Body
- ● Leg Area

# Danger Points

I would like to mention right up front that I think there are three danger points when using a chainsaw.

- **Danger No. 1: The Saw.**
- **Danger No. 2: The Tree.**
- **Danger No. 3: You.**

We have already discussed the frequency and seriousness of chainsaw accidents, that in a recent year more than 26,000 chainsaw injuries were treated in hospital emergency rooms, and the fact that it takes 110 stitches to close the typical chainsaw wound. There is no question that the chainsaw is a dangerous tool. However, you might be surprised to learn that although eighty-five percent of **injuries** come from contact with the moving chain, ninety percent of **deaths** related to chainsaw accidents are caused by trees or branches falling on the chainsaw operator or on bystanders.

Trees and parts of trees are large, heavy, and unpredictably springy. A large limb weighs several hundred pounds and a tree trunk might weigh several tons. A limb that is bent under the weight of the fallen tree can spring free with deadly force. For this reason it's important that you learn to tell when a tree is leaning (page 110), what is a widow-maker (it's any chunk of tree that might break loose while you're standing underneath), how to read the tension in a limb, how to plan an escape route (page 111), and what is the correct sequence to follow when you want to fell a tree (page 113).

> ⚠️ **CAUTION**
>
> It's physically demanding to work with a chainsaw, so you need to take breaks often and stop when you are tired. With the physical work of sawing while wearing a full kit of safety gear, heat stress may also become a risk. Drink plenty of liquids, stop to cool down, and plan your work for the coolest part of the day.

A widowmaker is any large, broken limb high up in a tree, so-called because when you start to work on the tree, the limb is liable to bust loose and fall. The wind blew this one down just two days after the first photo was taken. Anyone underneath would have been severely injured, if not killed. More on page 164.

As for you, a casual attitude about chainsaw safety is perhaps your biggest risk. By this I mean you deciding for whatever reason that you can do without your personal protective equipment. You deciding that you are fit enough to hoist a heavy saw all day long, without stopping to rest. You deciding you can continue working even when the daylight has faded into dusk, and even though you're tired, hot, and thirsty. You deciding that you are immune to the risks, and exempt from safe practices. You forgetting even for a moment that you yourself are responsible for not hurting yourself or anyone else with your chainsaw.

As for me, I find that taking the time to put on my safety gear helps me anchor my attitude in the safety zone and focus on what I'm doing.

## Sawing Overhead

It's very tempting to reach overhead to cut low limbs and branches from the tree trunk. There are two problems. The first problem is, the branch may suddenly break free and fall on you. If you are on a ladder, it will knock you off. The other problem is, the end of the branch may start dropping well before you sever it completely. When the tips of the branches hit the ground, the supple young growth may behave like a spring, propelling the whole limb back toward the tree trunk. And that is where you are standing—or perched up on your ladder. Down you go, with a running chainsaw in your hand. Not good!

To remove low branches, use a hand-powered bow saw (page xx). For overhead work, try a pole saw or a long-handled pair of loppers (see Chapter 5, Project 4, page 100).

## THE RULES

I have a few safety rules that I always follow. There are only five of them. I agree that lists of rules are tedious and boring, but this is a chainsaw we're talking about. Please read and think about these five rules.

- **Rule No. 1:** It's smart, not wussy, to know your own limits and know when to call in a professional. The cost of the pro will always be less than the cost of an accident. A lot less.

- **Rule No. 2:** Do not work without personal protective equipment. Just don't. Take the time to put it on especially when it is only a few cuts. If the weather is too hot for safety gear, it's too hot for you to work. Maybe start again in the cool of the early morning.

- **Rule No. 3:** Do not attempt anything that you aren't sure about. You can always shut off the saw to plan the sequence of cuts and rehearse the moves. Make sure you understand when and where that heavy limb is liable to fall, and how you won't be in its path.

- **Rule No. 4:** Keep two hands on the handles of the running saw. If you need to use one hand for something else, first shut the saw off and put it down on the ground. You can't cut your hands when they're wrapped around the saw's handle, and you're much less likely to lose control of the saw.

- **Rule No. 5.** Don't climb in a tree if you can avoid it. If you do climb in a tree, do not take the chainsaw with you. A corollary to this rule is, do not use a chainsaw to cut over your head or while standing on a ladder.

# PERSONAL PROTECTIVE EQUIPMENT

The greatest percentage of injuries is to the left leg and left hand. Chainsaw-proof gloves and leg protection will cut your risk by more than half. Even if you never cut your chaps, they can pay for themselves in the oily dirt and wear-and-tear they will save on your pants. A helmet with visor and faceshield will help protect your face and head from the most disfiguring injuries and gives me a sense of security. Quality steel-toed chainsaw boots can last a lifetime.

The total cost of a safety package ($300–$400) can be more than the chainsaw, but it is cheap insurance: the medical costs of an average chainsaw accident, based on a 2000 study of insurance claims, was $12,000.

- **Hardhat/hearing protection/ mesh visor:** $50
- **Safety glasses:** $5
- **Leg protection:** $60
- **Work boots:** $100
- **Kevlar-padded work gloves:** $25
- **Upper-body protection** (optional, but recommended): $100

These protective items dramatically reduce your risk of injury. Would you drive your car without wearing your seatbelt? The same can be said of operating a chainsaw without the proper protective gear.

Have you ever seen a neighbor using a chainsaw in the backyard without chaps, helmet, or foot protection? It would be interesting to know how many emergency room visits were by chainsaw users wearing shorts and tennis shoes.

Personal protective equipment (PPE) is one area homeowners seem to ignore. Even if you follow all of the recommendations for safe cutting, and take every precaution, accidents do happen. Good equipment can protect you.

Face shield (or goggles) · Hard hat · Hearing protection · Work gloves · Chaps (or other leg protection) · Steel-toed boots

Jen is dressed for yard work with a 14-inch chainsaw. She's planning to fell a small tree, then limb and buck it on the ground. Her personal protective equipment: hard hat with mesh face shield and hearing protection, work gloves, Kevlar chaps for leg protection, and steel-toed work boots.

Chainsaw (or forestry) jacket

Brian plans to fell, limb, and buck a large tree with an 18-inch saw. He's wearing the same set of personal protective equipment as Jen (above), plus a chainsaw jacket (sometimes called a forestry jacket) for upper body protection. The orange yoke is reinforced with Kevlar. A jacket like this is hot in summer, but vests offering similar protection are available for about the same price, $100. Compare this to the medical costs of an average chainsaw accident: $12,000, based on a 2000 study of insurance claims.

## Controlling the Chainsaw

To learn how to control the chainsaw, consider the forces involved.

- The chain on the top of the bar races away from the operator.
- The chain on the bottom of the bar speeds toward the operator.
- The chain travels downward as it changes direction around the nose of the saw bar.

Remembering high-school physics, for every action there is an equal but opposite reaction. As a result:

- When you are cutting downward using the chain on the bottom of the guide bar, the forces pull the saw in toward the wood, and/or the wood toward the operator.
- When you are cutting upward using the chain on the top of the bar, the forces push the wood and the saw engine away from one another.
- You don't cut with the nose of the bar. If you did, the forces would tend to rotate the saw upward—that's kickback.

Controlling the chainsaw requires planting both feet on the ground in a sturdy marching stance and keeping both hands on the saw handles. Whether cutting downward or upward, keeping the saw engine close to the wood helps you control the forces of pull-in and push-back.

As the chain rounds the nose of the guide bar, its motion suddenly acquires a downward component. As a result, when the upper quadrant of the bar nose contacts the wood, it's liable to be thrown upward. The saw abruptly pivots in your hands in a direction you weren't braced to resist— that's kickback as well.

## Reading the Tree

Because of gravity, heavy stuff—like trees and tree limbs—tends to fall down. A leaning tree tends to fall in the direction of the lean, and a log lying on a slope tends to roll downhill. Common sense informs you and guides you to be out of the tree's path.

The energy in living wood is another thing. Wood is supple, and it will bend a long way before it breaks. A limb that is bent under the weight of a fallen tree may pack a tremendous amount of force. The chainsaw operator must learn how to read these forces to predict the behavior of a sprung limb when it's suddenly cut free. There are three different situations to look out for:

- **Free limb.** When you cut into the limb, is it free to fall? Will the falling limb close up on the chainsaw bar, trapping it in the wood? Or will the sawn limb fall easily away? Where will you be— underneath the falling limb, or safely out of the way?
- **Sprung limb.** Is the limb trapped and bent (sprung) between the weight of the tree trunk and the ground? When you cut into the limb, is it liable to recoil violently? Which way will it go? Where will you be—in the path of the flying wood, or safely on the other side of the tree trunk?
- **When you remove a limb from a downed tree**, what's left to hold the heavy trunk up off the ground? Is it going to drop straight down, or is it going to pivot unpredictably on the remaining limbs? Where will you be—in the path of the dropping or rolling wood, or safely out of the way?

## FREE LIMB

When the tree limb is not sprung and has a clear path to fall to the ground, it's best to sever it with two cuts. This is true whether the tree is standing or lying on the ground. Make the first cut upward and go a third of the way into the wood. Make the second cut downward, aiming for the first cut. If you were to cut downward in the first place, the limb likely would splinter and fall without being severed. If you were to try and sever it with the upward cut, the limb's weight likely would trap the saw bar in the cut.

Cut upward...

...cut downward...

... the limb falls to the ground.

## TRAPPED LIMB

The bent limbs in this photo are holding the tree trunk up off the ground. If I were to cut into these limbs, they would spring. So I don't cut them yet. Instead, I remove the unsprung limbs from the top side, then buck the trunk from the small end back toward the butt. When I return to the sprung limbs, there's not much trunk left. The less weight, the less springing force when you do release the supporting limbs.

Bent limbs support trunk.

Cut the unsprung limbs.

Buck the log.

# Kickback

Kickback causes many chainsaw accidents. Kickback can occur whenever the upper part (quadrant) of the tip of the guide bar has contact with, but does not cut through, an obstacle while the chain is moving. The chain is moving away from the operator at that point, so contact transfers the power to the bar, which quickly propels the guide bar upward and backward in an uncontrolled arc—often right toward the operator.

Kickback can happen with lightning speed. With a saw at full throttle, the chain can reach speeds upwards of seventy miles per hour. This speed, transformed to the saw's rotation, means the tip of the bar can reach the operator in $^{15}/_{100}$ of a second. No one can react that quickly and an accident is very likely to happen.

The chain brake was designed to prevent such accidents from happening. An inertial chain brake (sometimes called an "automatic chain brake") can stop the chain in $^{5}/_{100}$ of a second. A manual chain brake that must be pushed forward with the left hand can stop the chain in $^{11}/_{100}$ of a second. It is easy to see the importance of these safety features.

## Avoiding kickback

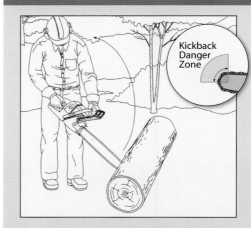

Most chainsaw accidents result from kickback: when the upper part of the guide bar tip—known as the kickback danger zone—contacts any solid object, the guide bar will jump back toward the operator.

Although some chainsaws have safety features to prevent kickback, handling the saw correctly is the best insurance. Always be aware of the guide bar tip's location, and never cut with the tip. Watch for objects behind the one you are cutting; such hazards may be obscured by branches or leaves.

## Three (staged) photos show how kickback happens:

After touching the upper tip of the guide bar, the kickback motion has started.

The downward motion of the chain around the saw nose starts the saw rotating clockwise.

The speeding chain may strike the operator in the head or shoulder. The saw in this photo is turned off.

## ⊗ KICKBACK PROBLEM:

Kickback occurs if there is an unexpected or sudden contact with wood in the upper quadrant of the bar nose.

This saw is liable to kick back when the upper part of the tip meets the wood.

## ✓ KICKBACK SOLUTION:

Pay attention to where the bar nose is. The upper quadrant of the tip should not be touching the wood. And cut with full throttle in a slow, steady, controlled motion.

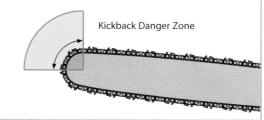

Kickback Danger Zone

## ⊗ KICKBACK PROBLEM:

If you stand directly in line with the guide bar, and your saw does kick back, you are almost guaranteeing an accident.

## ✓ KICKBACK SOLUTION:

Always position yourself so you are not in line with the guide bar, as shown at left below. If the saw does kick back for whatever reason (center photo), it will bypass your head and shoulders (right).

Stand off slightly to the side of the cut.

A saw can kick back so quickly that you will not have time to react.

If you are standing to the side, the saw will bypass your head and shoulders. The saw in this photo is turned off.

## ❌ KICKBACK PROBLEM:

Kickback can occur when the cutters of the chain bite too much wood and cannot cut it. Two things can cause this:

- The depth gauges in the chain are too low, exposing too much cutter. (See the sharpening information in Chapter 6, page 168.)

- The depth gauges are not rounded, causing them to bite.

## ✅ KICKBACK SOLUTION:

- Use a depth-setting gauge to file the depth gauges (See Chapter 6.)

- Round off the depth gauges.

- Have your chainsaw sharpened by a professional.

## ❌ KICKBACK PROBLEM:

Kickback can occur if you strike a branch that can move, a small twig, rock, or nail.

Cutting small branches that move when the saw hits them can cause kickback.

## ✅ KICKBACK SOLUTION:

Do not cut small branches that can move unless you can reach the stable base of the branch where it meets the tree trunk.

Kickback is less likely if you trim small branches near the tree trunk.

Tip can contact trunk. Better to turn around and cut from other side, as shown above.

**WRONG!**

### ⚠ WARNING

**Avoid situations that can cause kickback:**

Top or blade nose touches bottom or side of kerf during reinsertion

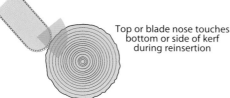

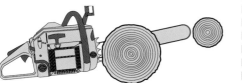

Blade nose strikes another object

### ⚠ WARNING

**Protecting yourself from kickback:**

- Keep your left arm as straight as possible.
- Keep your left hand behind the guard/chain brake.
- Keep your left thumb wrapped opposite your fingers.
- Do not stand directly in line with the guide bar but slightly to the left.
- Wear your personal protective equipment.

# Pull-In

If you are cutting on the bottom of the guide bar (the section of chain that is returning to the saw head), the force tends to pull the saw and the operator in toward the wood, or vise-versa This is called pull-in and can happen quickly. The operator may be pulled off balance, the wood might be thrown back at the operator, or the saw may be pulled forward, inadvertantly contacting something, causing kickback.

### ❌ PULL-IN PROBLEM:

When cutting with the bottom of the bar on the top of a log, the natural reactive force tends to pull the saw in toward the wood.

Pull-in occurs when cutting on the bottom, far end of the bar. It can happen quickly enough to pull the operator off balance, losing control of the saw.

### ✅ PULL-IN SOLUTION:

To prevent pull-in, work with the saw head close to the wood you are cutting.

Work with the saw head (not the tip) close to the wood. Always cut at full throttle and push down slowly enough to keep the engine and chain speed high. This cuts the wood rather than "biting" it.

# Push-Back

Push-back happens when you are cutting from below, using the chain on the top of the guide bar. This chain is moving away from the saw head. You often need to do this when cutting limbs from a tree (page 126). The force of the moving chain pushes the saw and the operator away from the wood you are cutting. The problem is that if the force pushes the guide bar completely out of the wood, the chainsaw can kick back into the operator. As the bar leaves the cut, if the upper quadrant of the bar nose contacts the wood, the push-back will turn into a kickback.

## ✖ PUSH-BACK PROBLEM:

When cutting on the underside of a log (with the top of the bar), the saw wants to quickly push away from the wood.

Push-back occurs when cutting on the top of the bar. If not controlled, the bar nose can contact the wood, leading to kickback.

## ✔ PUSH-BACK SOLUTION:

- Always cut at full throttle and ease into the cut so the chain is less likely to catch the wood.

- Do not cut with the upper end (nose) of the bar.

- Keep your left hand thumb wrapped tightly around the top handle and behind the front guard/chain brake, in position to activate the brake automatically. See top photo.

- Position your body to the left of the line of cut. See bottom photo. Then, if there is a kickback, the bar and chain will pass to the right of you.

Wrapping your left thumb around the top handle ensures a firm grip and greater control, and allows the chain brake to operate in the event of kickback.

Stand firmly with legs slightly separated and to the left of the cut line.

# Pinch

Pinch can be one of the most frustrating problems when cutting with a chainsaw. It happens when the saw's guide bar and chain literally get pinched in the wood (right). A pinched chain can also push back and kick back.

> ## ⚠ CAUTION
>
> When trying to remove a pinched guide bar, do not use a second chainsaw to "cut out" the first one. The second saw can get pinched or damaged when it hits the first saw. Also, do not try to pull, twist, or force the saw out as this could cause damage to the bar and chain. There is a "correct" way to free a pinched saw using a second saw—see page 24.

How does pinch happen? Often it is when cutting down on a section of log that is supported on both ends (below). A log that is supported this way is under a lot of compression stress on the top side and tension stress on the bottom side. As you cut down from the top, the center of the log will drop before it is cut completely through. This closes up the kerf and pinches the bar and chain.

The guide bar is pinched halfway through the cut. Tugging on the saw to free the bar has pulled the chain out of the bar slot.

This log is supported by brush on both ends and a prime candidate for pinching the guide bar.

## Making angled bucking cuts

When a section of trunk is balanced in such a way that one cut section is likely to remain stationary while the other falls toward the guide bar, make the two bucking cuts at an angle to prevent pinch.

Make the first cut from the top, angling it downward toward the section of the tree that will remain stationary. Saw one-third of the way through the trunk. To sever the pieces, cut up from underneath at about the same angle.

## ❌ PINCH PROBLEM:

When cutting down into a log supported on both ends, the kerf closes up and pinches the bar in place.

## ✅ PINCH SOLUTION:

The best solution is to lift the branch or log to relieve the pinch and then remove the saw. Shut the saw off, then use a second tree branch or sturdy sapling as a lever to lift the log and relieve the tension, as shown at left.

Next, carefully lift out the pinched saw, left.

As a last resort, you can use another saw to cut near the original cut to free the pinched saw. Make a small cut down from the topside about one foot away from the pinched saw, below left.

Make a cut up from the bottom of the branch or log to meet the small top cut, below center.

The shorter log should fall away easily. With the pressure off the bar, the pinched saw can be lifted out of the kerf, below right.

Recruit a friend with a strong back to fit a pry pole under the problem log.

As your helper lifts the pry pole, carefully remove the saw straight out of the kerf.

Staying clearly away from the pinched saw, make a small top cut down from the top.

Align the bottom cut with the small top cut.

The small, lightweight log will fall away, freeing the saw.

## ❌ PINCH PROBLEM:

When felling a tree or cutting down a stump, the kerf closes up and pinches the bar in place.

When cutting down the stump shown in Chapter 5, the guide bar became pinched in the kerf.

## ⚠ WARNING

If your saw becomes pinched while you are making the felling (back) cut, you know that the tree has started leaning the wrong way, and is now in danger of falling the wrong way. Use the pull rope, if you had the foresight to place one in the tree, to correct the lean toward the direction of fall. If no rope is in place, pound wedges into the cut to correct the lean. If you don't have a rope in place, or wedges at hand, then you must call a professional for help. Keep yourself and everyone else far away, because the tree may fall at any time. You are in a very dangerous situation, without the tools to extricate yourself.

## ✅ PINCH SOLUTION:

Shut the saw off. If the guide bar is in far enough to allow it, drive one or two wedges in behind the bar to free the saw.

I placed a wedge in the kerf and tapped it in with an ax. The saw itself is hidden behind the trunk in this photo.

The wedge opened up the kerf enough for me to withdraw the bar, start the saw, and finish the cut.

I have already mentioned the importance of preventing kickback in this chapter, and I will be mentioning it a number of times throughout this book. And most owner's manuals will spend pages on it. That is because it is probably going to happen to you. I know of few chainsaw operators who do not have at least one kickback story.

Manufacturers have developed features such as safety chain and bars, chain brakes, and tip guards, but there are still thousands of kickback injuries every year. Kickback is like lightning—it strikes without warning and is faster than human reflexes can react.

A millwright and part-time chainsaw operator who suffered a severe chest wound from a kickback invented the Centurion Safety Guard. His invention took a different approach to the problem in the hope it would spare others from such an injury. The Centurion will not prevent kickback, but it does provide a barrier between the operator and the cutting chain.

The system is remarkably simple, inexpensive, and lightweight. It is based around a solid steel alloy bar attached under the bolts holding the sprocket cover plate. The flat steel bar extends nearly the length of the guide bar and chain, and about two inches above the top of the chain. In the event of a kickback, you would be struck by this metal bar instead of by the chain, thus protecting you from being cut.

The bar is spring-loaded and a hinge allows it to be in its safety position for normal cutting (see top photo) or locked upright at ninety degrees for undercutting (see photo at right) or to allow cleaning and chain sharpening.

Safeguard Ventures (*www.SafeguardVentures.com*) manufactures the Centurion in two sizes to fit nearly every saw with a bar length of fourteen to twenty-two inches and two bar studs on the right-hand side of the saw. As Safeguard says, "It only needs to work once."

Top cutting with Centurion in safety position.

Undercutting with Centurion in the up position.

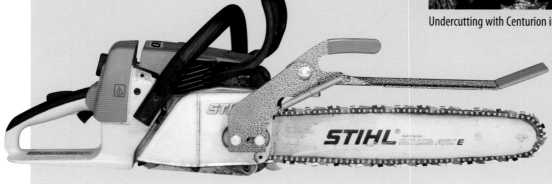

The Centurion Safety Guard can easily be added to most chainsaws.

## FINAL THOUGHTS

Let me leave this safety chapter with a couple of thoughts:

**If you are new to using a chainsaw, start small.** Cutting a downed tree for firewood (bucking, see Chapter 5 on pages 72–83), or taking the limbs off a small tree that is already down (see Chapter 5 on pages 126–133), would be a good place to start. If you feel you must fell a tree, select a small one. Or better yet, find a short stump left over from a tree someone else has already cut down and use that for practice. You can make all of the same cuts in it; you just will not have the weight of a whole tree to worry about.

**Never, ever leave a running chainsaw unattended.** Kids, animals, and nosy neighbors are extremely curious.

**Do not work alone.** Whether it is out in the woods or just in the backyard, have someone with you. But having said that, there are two things both you and your friend should know:

- He/she should never be too close to you as you work with a chainsaw. Close enough to keep an eye on you, but far enough away to stay out of danger. (When felling a tree, that is two tree lengths away.)

- Never have your friend hold a piece of wood while you cut it. (For that matter, never hold a piece of wood yourself with one hand and try to cut it using a chainsaw with the other.)

Finally, know when you are out of your league. If the job is too big, or dangerous, (or you are not even sure whether it is too big or dangerous), call in a professional tree service (see Chapter 5, Project 12, pages 164–167).

Enough said, for now.

## Transporting Your Saw

A chainsaw can be dangerous to transport—even when it is not running. Whenever you are carrying your saw to or from a worksite, observe the following rules:

- Turn off the engine.

- Engage the chain brake.

- Carry with the saw pointed behind you.

- Use a scabbard or a proper case (see photos.)

- Never transport in the passenger compartment of a vehicle.

- Secure with rope, bungee cords, or straps.

- If transported in a trunk, secure with the fuel cap facing up and remove the saw from the vehicle as soon as possible to prevent accumulation of fumes.

- And, of course, store the chainsaw out of reach of children.

When walking with your saw, keep the chain bar covered and facing backward.

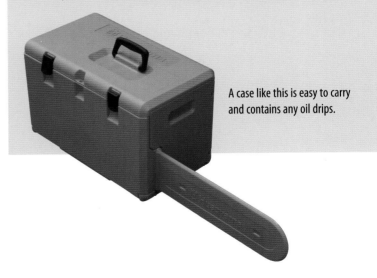

A case like this is easy to carry and contains any oil drips.

# CHAPTER 2

# Buying a Chainsaw
## Which Is the Best One for You?

**B**uying a chainsaw is a lot like buying a new vehicle. It is a good idea to make a number of decisions and narrow your options even before you head out to the dealer. If it is a new vehicle, you have to decide if you are looking for a standard family car, a sports car, a truck, a van, an SUV, or maybe even a Hummer. As far as a saw goes, maybe you do not even need a chainsaw. Perhaps a bow saw, hedge trimmer, or loppers will work (more on that in Chapter 5, Projects 4 and 5).

When you are taking down branches more than two to three inches in diameter, cutting up logs for firewood, or taking down a whole tree, a chainsaw is probably the best choice. It is the quickest, and, if used correctly, the safest tool for the job.

There are many options in brands, styles, and sizes of chainsaws available at most retail dealers.

# Electric vs. Gas-Power

If you have decided you need a chainsaw, what is the first decision you will have to make? I would recommend first determining if an electric or gasoline-powered saw best suits your needs. Both will cut wood, but comparing the two is like comparing apples to oranges.

## ELECTRIC CHAINSAWS

### Pros:

- **Less expensive.** An electric saw can be purchased for as little as $30. (But you generally get what you pay for!)

- **Lightest in weight.** This makes electric saws easier to use for smaller operators. You can work with them longer without becoming tired.

- **No fuel.** Simply plug them in without worrying about the fuel/oil mixture of gas saws.

- **Easy to start.** Simply squeeze an electric switch.

- **Quieter.** They are easier on the ears (and the nerves).

- **No fumes.**

- **Less maintenance.** No spark plugs, air filters, or fuel filters to change.

- **Can be used indoors.**

### Cons:

- **Slower cutting.** The chain rotates at about half the chain speed of a gas saw.

- **Limited cutting range.** You must be near an electric outlet or the length of your extension cords.*

- **Must plug into** a GFCI outlet or cord.

- **Potential electric shock hazard.** Be sure the motor is double insulated and the cord is grounded with a three-prong plug. Do not work in the rain or wet conditions. Be aware of where the power cord is at all times when cutting.

- **Shorter length bar** (four-and-one-half to eighteen inches), due to limited power, restricts size of wood that can be cut.

- **No chain brake.** Increased risk of injury if something goes wrong.

- **Manual bar oiler.** Operator must remember to use thumb-operated oil pump, or chain may overheat and break.

- **Close and limited grip top handles.** Handle geometry can reduce control and restrict some cutting angles.

*Battery powered saws are becoming more popular and will become more powerful in the future. Generally, they are equipped with a very short bar so they are limited to occasional use for cleaning up wind damage, tree pruning, and small cutting.

This 24 volt cordless Hyundai chainsaw has a 9" chain bar.

## GAS-POWERED CHAINSAWS

| Pros: | Cons: |
|---|---|
| ■ **Faster cutting.** Higher chain speed. The chain can rotate up to seventy mph, which means more work can be done in less time. | ■ **Generally more expensive.** With more speed and power comes more expense. But it is usually worth it. |
| ■ **Range of choices and cutting capacity.** From six pounds in weight up to forty pounds. With twelve-inch-long bars up to six-foot-long bars. | ■ **Fuel/Oil mixtures.** Gas-powered saws require special fuel/oil mixtures that can be expensive and time consuming (see Chapter 4 pages 58–60). |
| ■ **Work anywhere.** Because you are not tied to an electric cord, gas-powered chainsaws can work in just about any kind of environment (except indoors), and there is no concern of cutting the cord or electric shock. | ■ **Starting.** Starting a gas-powered saw involves a number of steps (see Chapter 4, pages 64–69). |
| ■ **More safety features and available after-market attachments.** Since gas-powered saws are generally considered the standard in the industry, you are more likely to find built-in safety features such as chain brakes and accessories to make them easier and safer to use. | ■ **Weight.** Because gas-powered saws are usually larger, and they have large motors, longer bars, a tank full of fuel, and a tank of oil, they can be more tiring to use, especially for a small operator. |
| | ■ **Noisier and create fumes.** Less friendly to the operator or the environment. |
| | ■ **More maintenance.** Spark plugs and air and fuel filters need regular attention. |

## A good place to start...and to stay

You can get the feel of a chainsaw by cutting firewood on a saw buck using an electric saw. So, whatever your ultimate plans, that's a good place to start. And you will find that you can maintain a wooded suburban yard up to a half-acre using an electric chainsaw. Compared to gas saws, electrics are easier to use and to maintain, and less expensive too.

## Lefties

Chainsaws pose special challenges for left-handed people. They were designed for right-handed use, and no manufacturer currently offers a left-handed model. Swapping hands—that is, gripping the back handle with the left hand and the top handle with the right—puts the left-handed user closer to the chain and increases the risk of injury. Chainsaws with full-wrap front handles are easier for lefties to use, but at the cost of not having either hand behind the manual chain brake.

The best advice might be to learn how to hold the saw the same way a right-hander would. That's the only way all of the saw's safety features would come into play.

For a left-handed starter pull in the kneeling position, try using the heel and not the toe to stabilize the saw.

# Engine and Guide Bar

Chainsaws are made of two main parts: a power head (engine) and the cutting system (chain and guide bar). To make matters a little confusing, power heads come in a variety of sizes and bars come in a variety of lengths.

To make it easier, when buying from larger retail centers, the manufacturer usually matches the guide bar length to the power head. It seems they will often match a power head with the longest bar it is capable of using, perhaps to maximize the saw's usefulness. But what you really should be considering, in both the size of the engine and the guide bar, is the size wood you will be cutting most commonly. Although a larger saw will cut smaller wood, you'll be doing so at the expense of energy and safety.

## ENGINE SIZE

The larger saw will use more gas, and the extra bar length may increase your risk of kickback.

Another important consideration is the weight of the saw, versus your physical condition. Limbing and bucking a downed tree can be a half-day's work. The saw you can easily heft at the dealership is going to become very heavy, and more difficult for you to control, by the end of the day. The work will go better, and you will be safer, if you match the size of the engine and bar to the work you will be doing, and don't worry about extra capacity for bigger tasks that rarely, if ever, are necessary.

Do not let bar length alone be the determining factor in selecting a chainsaw. Let's start with the engine. With electric saws, the size is described in terms of horsepower. Typical horsepower for a homeowner's electric saw might be anywhere from one horsepower to three horsepower. Some manufacturers also give the horsepower of their gas-powered saws, but more typically, they are measured in cubic inches (ci) or centimeters (cc), which denotes engine displacement for a homeowner's saw would be 1.5ci to 4ci (30cc to 64cc).

It would naturally follow that the bigger the saw's engine, the more power it will have, and the quicker it will cut. However, the larger the saw, the heavier, more cumbersome and tiring it will be to use. For this reason it is important to choose a saw that will fit both the user and the job being done. The chart at left includes a variety of tasks and the recommended engine sizes.

## Engine Size

| Task | Recommended Engine Size |
|------|------------------------|
| Trimming/Removing a hedge (requires comb attachment) | 30cc/small electric |
| Pruning trees | 30cc/small electric |
| Limbing | 30cc/mid-size electric |
| Small tree felling | 30–40cc/mid to large electric |
| Light firewood cutting (under 10" diameter) | 35–45cc/large electric |
| Moderate size tree felling | 45cc+/large or pro electric |
| Medium firewood cutting (10" to 16" diameter) | 40–50cc/pro electric |
| Large log cutting (16" to 24" diameter) | 50cc+ |

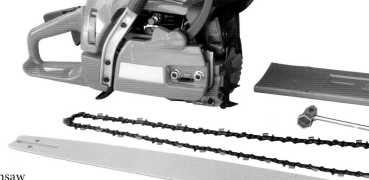

Typical Husqvarna saw with bar (foreground), chain (middle), scrench and scabbard, and power head (back).

## BAR LENGTH

When buying from a chainsaw dealer or store that specializes in outdoor equipment, you'll probably have a choice of bar length to go with the size power head you've chosen. A knowledgeable dealer will be able to suggest the proper match for your needs.

Bar length is measured from the cutting tip to where the chain enters the engine housing. Though the standard bar lengths on homeowner saws are fourteen inches, sixteen inches, eighteen inches, and twenty inches, bars can be as short as eight inches or as long as forty-two inches (but leave anything exceeding twenty inches to the pros). My preference is to put a shorter bar on whatever power head size I need. A shorter bar is lighter and easier to manipulate and less likely to reach beyond where I want it to, possibly contacting an object and causing kickback.

You may think that because you can cut from both sides of a log or tree trunk, a fourteen-inch-long bar can cut through a twenty-eight-inch diameter log. That may be, but there is something else to consider here. Is the engine powerful enough to cut through a twenty-eight-inch diameter log? And is it safe? What it takes is the correct combination of engine size and bar length to get the job done efficiently. For safest cutting, the bar should be two inches longer than the largest wood you intend to cut.

Ask your dealer for recommendations for the cutting you will be doing. He may even suggest a different combination if you are cutting hardwood as opposed to softwood.

| Guide Bar Length | |
| --- | --- |
| **Task** | **Recommended Bar Length** |
| **Trimming/Removing a hedge** | No more than 16" |
| **Pruning trees** | 12" or less |
| **Limbing** | 12"–14" |
| **Small tree felling** | 12"–14" |
| **Light firewood cutting** (under 10" diameter) | 14"–16" |
| **Moderate size tree felling** | 16"–18" |
| **Medium firewood cutting** | 16"–18" |
| **Large log cutting** | 18"+ |

# Recommended Features

By this point, you've probably made some big decisions—electric or gas-powered, engine size, and bar length. But just like shopping for a new car, optional features can really make the difference. In a car, for example, you may have the option of leather seats. For a chainsaw, it may be heated handles.

You should look for several features. Because of the potential for injury when using a chainsaw, many of these features are standard, but some are not. Below is a list of the features I would recommend. Don't be afraid to take this list with you when you go shopping!

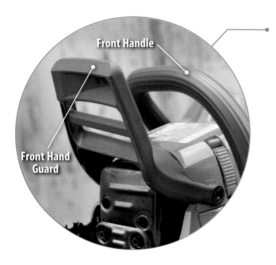

Front Handle

Front Hand Guard

## FRONT HAND GUARD
### Why is it important?

Like many power tools, chainsaws are designed for right-handed users. Your right hand controls the saw and throttle trigger by grabbing the rear handle. Your left hand grabs the handle on the top of the saw to control lateral movement and depth of cut. This leaves the left hand, nearest the moving chain, very exposed and unprotected. In the event of a kickback, the whole saw will rotate backwards. The **front hand guard** will help protect your left hand, wrist, forearm, and upper body.

Unfortunately for left-handers, chainsaws are not manufactured in left-handed configurations. Lefties should try holding a saw both ways, to learn which is more comfortable and gives the greatest control.

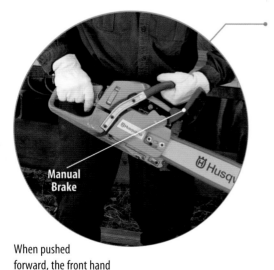

Manual Brake

When pushed forward, the front hand guard acts as the manual brake.

## CHAIN BRAKE
### Why is it important?

There are two types of **chain brakes**: manual and inertial. They are designed to stop a moving chain and help prevent injury. The front hand guard acts as a manual brake and as it is pushed forward by your hand it stops the chain in milliseconds. Pulling it back toward the handles allows the chain to resume movement. The inertial brake, which is built into the left-hand guard, acts on inertia alone. If there's a kickback, the inertial chain brake is designed to engage and stop the chain merely from the rotational motion of the saw. Your saw should have both a manual brake and an inertial brake.

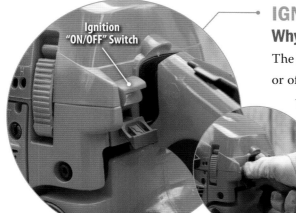

## IGNITION "ON/OFF" SWITCH
### Why is it important?

The **ignition "ON/OFF" switch** turns the electric system on or off. It must be clearly marked and should be located so that you can activate it (turn the saw off) without letting go of the rear handle. Check that your right hand thumb can easily reach the ignition switch.

## SAFETY THROTTLE
### Why is it important?

Your saw's throttle (trigger) should have a **safety throttle interlock/lockout**. This mechanism will not allow the trigger to be pulled unless you have a firm grip on the rear handle. Gripping the handle presses the safety throttle, allowing the trigger to be squeezed. It also prevents accidental chain acceleration if the trigger were to meet with a twig, branch, or similar object while the chainsaw engine was running.

## CHAIN CATCHER
### Why is it important?

Sometimes chains derail off the guide bar. And sometimes they break—at a very high speed. The **chain catcher** (aluminum finger in photo) is a protruding bar on the bottom of the saw that's designed to grab and stop the rotational motion of a chain that has become derailed or breaks.

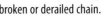

Scars caused by catching a broken or derailed chain.

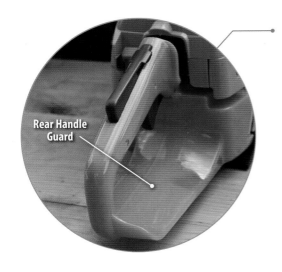

## REAR HANDLE GUARD
### Why is it important?

Even though the chain catcher will stop the rotation of a broken or derailed chain, it can still have enough motion to be thrown back at the operator. A widening of the back handle to become a **rear handle guard** is also designed to prevent injury to the hand. It can also aid in starting the chainsaw when held on the ground (see Chapter 4, pages 64–69).

## CHOKE
### What does it do?

Activating the **choke** (on some saws it pulls out, on others it is a toggle) restricts the air supply to the carburetor, making the fuel-air mixture rich. This helps start a cold engine, but leaving the choke closed once the engine begins to fire is liable to flood it with fuel and cause it to stall. On most saws, you set the choke and pull the starter rope until the engine first begins to cough. Then you open the choke and start the engine by pulling the rope one more time.

## ANTI-VIBRATION SYSTEM
### Why is an AV system important?

While cutting with a chainsaw, there is a lot of vibration that can lead to a very unpleasant and numbing effect on the hands or even to carpal tunnel syndrome. Most people can't hold a saw for more than a few seconds without an **anti-vibration system**. (It is sometimes called an Anti-Vibe or AV system.) These systems are made up of either rubber bushings or coil springs between the engine and handles.

## MUFFLER AND SPARK ARRESTOR
### Why is it important?

A **muffler** should reduce the engine's noise to acceptable levels and it should direct fumes away from the operator. In addition, the muffler should have a **spark arrestor** screen. The screen is designed to keep sparks from being ejected and thus prevent fires. The muffler itself will run hot enough to burn you—be careful!

## CORRECT CHAIN/BAR COMBINATIONS
### Why is it important?

All manufacturers will specify or supply the **correct chain** to fit on the **guide bar** of each of their saws. Using an incorrect combination may mean the chain will not fit the drive sprocket of the saw or the sprocket tip of the guide bar. This can lead to damage and a dangerous situation. If the length is incorrect, it will not fit on the saw or be able to be tensioned properly. Never use the wrong chain just because it is available.

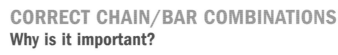

## BAR AND CHAIN SCABBARD
### Why is it important?

When transporting a chainsaw, it's easy to hurt yourself, the chain, or anything that encounters the chain if it's not properly covered. A **bar and chain scabbard** helps prevent this and keeps a sharp chain sharp. An alternative would be to use a saw case.

# Specialty Features

Once you are sure the chainsaw you are considering has the essential safety features, look at some of the other features that are available on many saws today. They are designed to make your job easier, more efficient, and, most important of all, safer.

### HEATED HANDLES
**What do they do?**

For extremely cold climates and winter cutting, **heated handles** not only add comfort but also can help reduce hand-arm-vibration syndrome. Unfortunately, it is a feature usually found only on mid-size and larger professional saws.

### BUMPER SPIKES/LOG CLAW/DOGS
**What do they do?**

**Bumper spikes** help pivot and stabilize the saw when sawing into large trunks and logs. Most saws have them either molded into the saw body or as a separate metal part, as shown here.

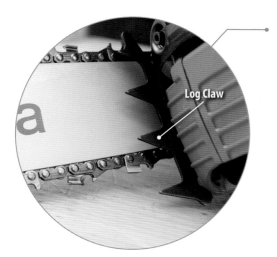

Log Claw

### DECOMPRESSION BUTTON
**What does it do?**

A **decompression button** releases cylinder pressure during starting. Because it reduces operator fatigue, it encourages easier starting.

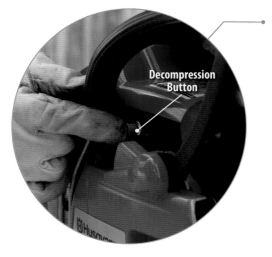

Decompression Button

### SPRING-LOADED STARTER HANDLE AND STARTER REELS
**What does it do?**

This is another feature that helps make starting easier. **Spring-loaded starter handle and starter reels** reduce shock to the hand and arm during start up.

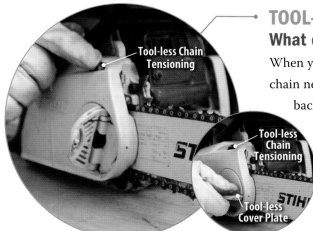

## TOOL-LESS COVER PLATE/CHAIN TENSION
### What do they do?

When you are out in the field or in the backyard and your chain needs a little adjustment, it is nice not to have to head back to your truck or into your shop to find the correct wrench. **Tool-less chain tensioning** allows you to tension your chain without the aid of any tools. The side-cover plate loosening, tightening, and chain tension adjusting can be done by hand. There are several types available; some tension the chain automatically.

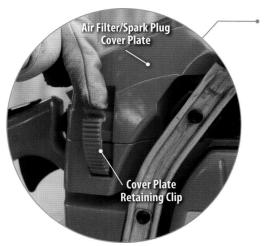

## TOOL-LESS AIR FILTER/ SPARK PLUG COVER PLATE
### What does it do?

The air filter is something you need to keep clean. A **tool-less air filter/spark plug cover plate** allows for easy access to both the air filter and the spark plug.

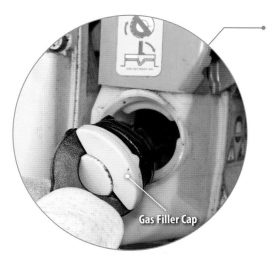

## QUICK RELEASE GAS AND OIL FILLER CAPS
### What do they do?

Sometimes it seems like I am spending as much time filling up my gas and oil tanks as I am sawing. **Quick release gas and oil filler caps** allow you to remove these caps with a mere quarter rotation without the use of tools.

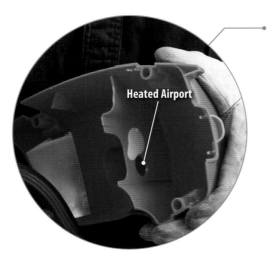

Heated Airport

## HEATED CARBURETOR
### What does it do?

One problem of working in freezing temperatures is the carburetor will freeze up. With a **heated carburetor**, a small plastic or rubber part can be moved or removed in the winter, allowing heated air to flow around the carburetor. Be sure this airway is not left open in the summer. A similar mechanism provides heat to the saw handle on some professional models.

Adjustable Oil Pump

## ADJUSTABLE OIL PUMP
### What does it do?

An **adjustable oil pump** allows fine tuning of the bar and chain oil system to provide proper lubrication and reduce waste.

## STRATIFIED SCAVENGING ENGINE
### What does it do?

Everyone is concerned about reducing harmful emissions and greenhouse gas. Two-cycle engines lose some unburned fuel/air mixture with exhaust gases during operation. A **stratified scavenging engine** (also known as strato-charged or X-torq) minimizes this loss by introducing clean air into the cylinder during operation. It can reduce harmful emissions by 60% and increase fuel economy by 20%. The feature will be standard on all chainsaws in the near future.

Engine Flywheel

Air Filter

## CLEAN AIR SYSTEM
### What does it do?

Named variously by different manufacturers, the **clean air system** uses the fins on the engine flywheel to propel larger dust and debris particles past the point where the saw inhales combustion air. This lengthens the intervals between air filter cleanings and replacements.

# Questions? Answers.

Before you head out to the dealer, ask yourself the following questions:

- **Where will you be cutting? Your backyard, in the open, in dense woods?** Many homeowners on a half-acre or less can reach everywhere with an electric chainsaw. If you have a larger property you most likely will need a gas saw. If you intend to travel off your own property with your gear, you should also have a chainsaw case to stay organized and transport safely.

- **How much weight are you comfortable lifting?** What is your level of fitness? Operating a chainsaw is tiring, and continuing to work when you are tired is very dangerous. A large, more powerful saw will speed the work, but it will require more energy and endurance. Size your saw not only in terms of the wood you'll be cutting, but also to your own physical attributes and limitations.

- **How much maintenance are you willing to do?** All saws require some maintenance—gas ones more than electrics. If you won't be doing maintenance, a good relationship with a local power equipment shop is your best bet.

- **What kind of wood will you be cutting?** Living white pine cuts a whole lot easier than dry white oak. One saw can do it all, but some wood will go a little faster.

- **What is the largest log you will be cutting?** The guide bar and saw motor should be matched to the size wood you will be cutting most often. The guide bar should be two inches longer than the largest diameter log. If you will be cutting large trees and sectioning them for firewood down to the smallest limbs, you soon will need two saws.

- **When does it make more sense to rent rather than buy a saw?** It depends on frequency of use. Once or twice a year, and you'll probably be better off to rent. If you don't have a place to store a saw, or don't want to fool with any kind of maintenance, then renting could be a good choice even for a more frequent user.

## Chain Basics

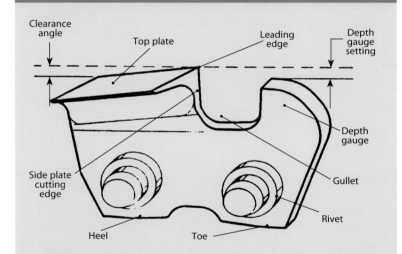

Saw chains have three significant dimensions: pitch, gauge, and the number of drive links. You must know all three to be sure a chain will fit your saw.

Pitch is the distance from one link to the next, typically 0.325 inch and ³⁄₈" on homeowner saws. Gauge is the thickness of the drive link as it enters the guide bar. Although there are four gauges available (.043, .050, .058, and .063), most saws use .050 gauge chain. The number of drive links relates to the length of the guide bar. A 14-inch bar typically has 52 drive links; you can always count the links in the old chain.

Big box stores sell guide bar and chain combination packs marked for the brand and model saw they will fit. When going to a dedicated saw shop, take the old chain. If you don't have one, take the saw and bar so the shop can match it.

# The Bottom Line

Obviously, you are going to have to choose the chainsaw and the dealer/retailer/seller that is best for your needs. It would be great to be able to have two or three saws with a number of bar lengths to choose from for different jobs. But unless you are a professional, that is probably not realistic. There is no perfect saw that will work in every situation.

Here are my recommendations:

| | |
|---|---|
| **"I'm going to use a chainsaw only once or twice."** | **Call a professional.** It will most likely be cheaper than buying the saw plus personal protective equipment. It doesn't matter whether you are a new user or a seasoned professional, an occasional user or a daily one—cutting trees with a chainsaw is dangerous and you must wear a helmet, face shield, eye protection, hearing protection, chaps, steel-toed boots, and leather gloves. |
| **"I'm a homeowner who needs to prune my bushes once a year and occasionally clean up some branches that have come down in the wind."** | **Choose a fourteen-inch gas saw, if you are likely to maintain it year-round; otherwise, choose an electric saw.** An unused, un-maintained gas saw probably will not start when you need it; the electric one will. Buy personal protective equipment along with your first saw: a helmet, face shield, eye protection, hearing protection, chaps, steel-toed boots, and leather gloves. |
| **"I am a part-time user who has access to some logs and want to cut my own firewood on a regular basis."** | **If you are not good with maintenance, choose a larger (sixteen-inch) electric saw.** The sacrifice in mobility and cutting speed will be made up by the ease of brushing it off and putting it away after each use. Next time you need it, simply plug it in, fill the oiler, and start cutting again.<br><br>**If you are looking for more cutting speed and freedom to roam untethered by an electric cord, choose a fourteen-inch or sixteen-inch gas saw.** Occasional users should add a stabilizer to the saw's gasoline, or use a premixed and stabilized fuel-oil combo. Gasoline rapidly goes bad and will gum up the saw's carburetor, frustrating all starting efforts.<br><br>**If you appreciate fine machinery and are prepared to maintain it, consider a professional-grade saw for the best power-to-weight ratio and performance.**<br><br>**Buy personal protective equipment along with your first saw:** a helmet, face shield, eye protection, hearing protection, chaps, leather gloves, and steel-toed boots. |
| **"I have some experience working with smaller chainsaws and now would like to try to make some income using a chainsaw."** | **If you are going to rely on your saw for income, invest in professional-grade equipment and realize that it will not be long before you need a second (backup) saw.** Consider having two different-sized saws so you can fit the tool to the task. Developing a relationship with a dedicated dealer will help ensure good and quick service when you need it. |

## DEDICATED DEALER

| Pros: | Cons: |
| --- | --- |
| ■ Knowledge | ■ More expensive |
| ■ Service-oriented | ■ May be limited choice of brands |
| ■ Parts and maintenance | |
| ■ Available accessories and safety gear | |
| ■ Knows local conditions | |
| ■ May be able to try a saw out before buying | |
| ■ Personal instruction available | |
| ■ Professional saws available | |
| ■ Wide selection of bars and power heads | |

## LARGE RETAILER
### (i.e. "Big Box" home improvement store)

| Pros: | Cons: |
| --- | --- |
| ■ Lower prices | ■ Limited sales staff knowledge |
| ■ May have wide selection of brands and models | ■ May not have a wide variety of bar lengths |
| ■ Convenience, immediate availability | ■ No in-house service after the sale |
| ■ May have accessories, apparel | ■ May be limited choice of parts |
| ■ Homeowner oriented | |

## INTERNET/CATALOG

| Pros: | Cons: |
| --- | --- |
| ■ Probably the lowest prices | ■ No one to answer questions or make recommendations |
| ■ No sales tax (depends on state) | ■ Shipping costs |
| ■ Research other users' opinions | ■ Shipping time |
| | ■ No local seller service after the sale |
| | ■ Can't try saw before buying |

## CLASSIFIED AD
### (used chainsaw)

| Pros: | Cons: |
| --- | --- |
| ■ Least expensive | ■ No returns |
| ■ Can try out before purchasing | ■ No parts or service after the sale |
| ■ Convenience | ■ Problems that previous owner doesn't tell you about |
| ■ No sales tax or shipping costs | ■ No warranty |
| | ■ Safety features absent on older saws |

## RENTAL AGENCY

| Pros: | Cons: |
| --- | --- |
| ■ Convenient | ■ Instruction or owner's manual may not be available |
| ■ Operating instruction should be available | ■ Renter is liable for any damage to the saw |
| ■ Good way to test a saw before buying one | ■ Saw may have been abused |
| ■ Saw is likely to be sharp and well maintained | |

# CHAPTER 3

# At the Store

## A Shopping List

To start and use a chainsaw, all you really need are some gas and oil (or an extension cord for an electric-powered saw). But to operate one safely, you need the correct and approved safety apparel. With personal protective equipment (PPE) in place, your risk of injury will be dramatically decreased. Think of these essential items as insurance to keep you out of the emergency room—or even worse. If you aren't willing to purchase personal protective equipment along with your saw, then you should skip the whole thing and hire a tree professional instead.

To keep your chainsaw running and working in the field, you will also need a basic tool kit. So, while you are at the store, pick up any of the following items you do not already have.

Before attempting your first chainsaw job, you will need various pieces of safety and other equipment, including a hard hat; hearing, face and eye protection; leather work gloves; steel-toe boots; Kevlar-reinforced chaps. Good dealers and some home centers can supply this gear.

# PERSONAL PROTECTIVE EQUIPMENT

☐ **Chaps/Leg Protection** — With Kevlar-type chain-stopping material.

☐ **Gloves** — Tight and close fitting, preferably including Kevlar-type material with protective guarding on the back of the left hand.

☐ **Protective Helmet/ Head Gear** — Adjustable for a good fit, with ear/hearing protection and a face shield (wire mesh screen or plastic).

☐ **Hearing Protection** — Earmuffs or earplugs if you are not using a helmet with built-in hearing protection. They should have a noise reduction rating of twenty-nine to thirty decibels.

☐ **Eye Protection** — Visor (on helmet) or safety glasses (both are best)

☐ **Work Boots** — Strong, steel-toed. Ideally with Kevlar or protective guarding on the top, tongue, and instep.

☐ **Upper Body Protection** — A jacket or vest with a Kevlar-reinforced shoulder yoke helps defend you from kickback injury.

## SERVICE AND MAINTENANCE TOOLS

❑ **Approved Gas Can with Gas** (see page 58)

❑ **Approved Two-Cycle Mix Oil** (see page 58)

❑ **Bar Oil**

❑ **Funnel**

❑ **Scrench or Socket Wrench and Screwdriver**
(for chain tensioning and spark plug removal/installation)

❑ **Box Wrenches** (to fit nuts and bolts on chainsaw)

❑ **Screwdrivers** (to tighten screws on chainsaw)
**Note:** Many saws use screws with uncommon heads.
A bit driver with interchangeable bits to fit the screws
on your saw may be needed.

❑ **Extra Spark Plug**

❑ **Spark Plug Gauge** (to check or set gap on spark plug)

❑ **Extra Air Filter**

❑ **Stiff Brush for Cleaning**

❑ **Rags for Cleaning**

## SHARPENING SUPPLIES

❑ **Round File** (properly sized for your chain)

❑ **Sharpening Guide** (for round file)

❑ **Flat File** (for filing the depth gauge on your chain)

❑ **Depth Setting Gauge** (for flat file)

| | | |
|---|---|---|
| ☐ | **Felling Wedges** | Minimum of two. Aluminum is preferred over plastic or steel. Plastic can chip and break or pop out of the cut if struck too hard. Steel can dull your chain if hit accidentally. |
| ☐ | **Ax** | A sharp ax is safer than a chainsaw for cutting very small branches off a tree trunk. It can also be used to drive wedges. |
| ☐ | **Sledgehammer** | Better than an ax for driving wedges. |
| ☐ | **Wood Splitter's Maul** | Better than an ax for splitting wood. |
| ☐ | **Cant Hook or Peavy** | Used to roll and move logs. |
| ☐ | **Timberjack** | Used to lift one end of a log for easier and safer bucking. |
| ☐ | **Throw Bag with Line** | Used to put a rope in a tree without climbing. |
| ☐ | **Rope** | For hand pulling to direct the fall of a tree. Should be three-eighths to one-half inch in diameter and twice as long as the tallest tree you plan to fell. |

## SAFETY EQUIPMENT

❏ **Cell Phone**

❏ **Fire Extinguisher**

❏ **Insect Spray**

❏ **First Aid Kit containing:**

    ❏ Band-Aids
    ❏ Latex Gloves
    ❏ Wound Cleaning Agents (such as moistened towelettes)
    ❏ Large Gauze Pads (at least eight by ten inches)
    ❏ Small Gauze Pads (four by four inches)
    ❏ Adhesive Tape
    ❏ Ace Bandage (roll of elastic wrap)
    ❏ Tweezers
    ❏ Scissors

# CHAPTER 4

# Getting Started
## Step-by-Step

**W**ith some power tools, you can open the box, plug it in or turn it on, and immediately go to work. Chainsaws are not quite that easy, though they are not that difficult either.

It is important that you read the owner's manual that comes with your new saw (as well as this book, of course!). That tree or log can wait. Reading the manual can keep you out of a lot of trouble right away. And, as discussed in Chapter 1, do not ignore safety information. In that regard, the most important factor is your own attitude. If you decide safety consciousness and personal protective equipment are for sissies, you are asking for trouble. But, if you accept that your chainsaw is potentially dangerous and challenging to operate, and you determine that you will do everything you can to use it safely and well, then you are likely to succeed.

Here's the three-point method for safely and securely holding a chainsaw when starting it: right foot on the rear handle, left hand on top handle, right hand pulls starter rope.

# Electric Chainsaws

It might seem that with an electric chainsaw all it would take is to plug it in, hit the trigger, and start cutting. There is a little more to it than that. Some models do come pre-assembled. But on others, you have to install the bar and chain.

This process should be described in the owner's manual and is generally the same as the gas-saw procedures on the following pages. The sequence usually involves loosening and removing the guide bar nuts and sprocket cover plate, and installing the guide bar onto the saw head. Then, the chain can be placed around the drive sprocket, along the top groove of the guide bar, and around the nose of the guide bar. (Make sure the cutting edges of the chain are facing in the right direction. That is, the cutting edges on top of the guide bar should be facing toward the nose.) Now the sprocket cover can be re-installed and the chain tensioned.

Even if your electric saw comes assembled, you should check the chain tension (page 56).

Your owner's manual should give you specific instructions on how to tension the chain and how much tension is appropriate

for your saw. The important thing is, the chain's drive links should not be able to be pulled out of the guide bar groove.

Even though an electric chainsaw does not use any fuel, you will need to add chain oil to the oil reservoir. The purpose of this is to keep the chain links lubricated as you are cutting. There is usually a thumb-operated oil pump you press before each cut that squirts oil onto the chain.

Your owner's manual should give you some guidance on the type of chain oil to use for different situations and temperatures. SAE #10, #30, or #40 motor oil would be typical. After filling the tank, be sure to tighten the cap firmly to avoid seepage. It is normal for oil to seep when the saw is not being used. Empty the oil tank after each use to avoid seepage.

The obvious disadvantages of an electric chainsaw is, you will need a GFCI-protected electrical outlet somewhere nearby, and that means an extension cord. Use only extension cords that are marked with the suffix W or W-A (example: SJTW or SJTW-A), designating them as being safe for outdoor use.

The other thing to consider is the size of the cord. This will vary based upon the power of your saw and the length of the cord. The cord must be heavy enough to carry the necessary current. An undersized

**⚠ CAUTION**

Unplug electric chainsaws from power source before adjusting chain tension.

Craftsman and Poulan both offer electric chainsaws with short, "pigtail" cords.

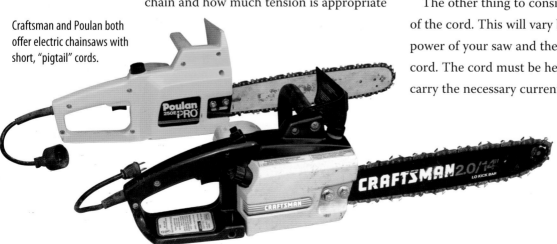

# Gas Chainsaws

cord will cause the voltage to drop at the saw. The motor loses power, overheats, and may fail.

Stamped on the extension cord should be an AWG (American Wire Gauge) number (Example: 16 AWG). The smaller the gauge number, the larger the wire. In your instruction manual, there should be a chart that lists the appropriate gauge number for the length of the extension cord to power your saw. For example, 16 AWG wire might be appropriate for a 50-foot cord, but if you need to use a 100-foot cord, it should be 14 AWG. Again, check your manual.

One other thing about electric chainsaws—and this may be obvious. At all times, know where your cord is positioned in relation to the cutting area. Make sure it is not hung up on branches, logs, or stumps. Many saws have an extension cord hitch designed into them to prevent the cord from coming loose. Use it.

And finally, inspect your cords often, looking for any damage. Electricity can be just as dangerous as an errant chainsaw.

## STARTING AN ELECTRIC SAW

An electric saw is far simpler to start than a gas saw. Follow these steps:

- Be sure bystanders are out of the way.
- Be aware of the power cord so you can avoid cutting into it.
- Fill the oil reservoir and check the chain tension.
- Before pulling the trigger switch to power up the saw, be sure the guide bar and chain are free of branches, twigs, wood, and your clothing.

Setting up and starting a gas-powered chainsaw involves a number of steps that must be followed in a logical order. If you have purchased a saw with its bar and chain off, or you are replacing your bar and chain for the first time, follow the steps on the next few pages to assemble and tension your saw, fill it with gas and oil, and safely start it.

### ⚠ CAUTION

Use protective gloves when assembling any gas or electric saw and handling chain. Cutting edges on chain are sharp.

### ⚠ CAUTION

Before working on your saw, be sure the ignition switch is set to the stop position or the "ON/OFF" switch to the off position, and disconnect the spark plug wire, too.

# Assemble Bar to Engine

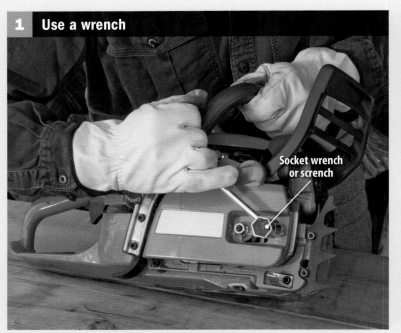

**1** **Use a wrench**

Socket wrench
or scrench

**2** **Remove cover plate**

Cover plate

**3** **Important components**

Drive sprocket
(behind clutch)

Oil slot

Chain
tensioning pin

## REMOVE COVER PLATE

**1 Use a wrench.** Use a properly sized socket wrench or scrench to remove the sprocket cover lug nut or nuts and cover plate from the studs.

**2 Remove cover plate.** Pull back the chain brake to disengage it. The cover plate can now be removed and set aside. Be sure to keep all parts logically organized for re-assembly later. Many saws come from the factory with plastic or cardboard packing spacers around the studs. Be sure to remove this packing material.

**3 Important components.** Inside you will find three important components: a drive sprocket (usually hidden behind the clutch, but sometimes the clutch is internal and the sprocket is visible), a chain-tensioning pin below the studs, and an oil hole or slot. The chain-tensioning pin may be on the inside of the cover plate. (Be sure to use the correct guide bar. Using a guide bar not made for your particular saw may result in misalignment of one of these parts.)

# Assemble Bar to Engine (continued)

## MOUNT CHAIN ON SPROCKET

**4 Locate drive sprocket.** On this saw, the drive sprocket is located behind the clutch. It may be a spur drive or a rim drive sprocket. If it is a rim drive, be sure the chain fits in the slots. Most importantly, the sharp edge of the teeth on the top run of chain should face forward, or the chain will be on backward. Finally, make sure the chain is on top of the chain catcher.

## SET BAR ON STUDS

**5 Position guide bar.** Use a screwdriver to adjust the tensioning pin as far back as possible to reduce chain tension. Position the correct guide bar in place and set it over the two studs.

**6 Slide guide bar.** Slide the guide bar back toward the drive sprocket.

## PLACE CHAIN IN SLOT

**7 Place chain links.** Place the chain drive links in the slot on top of the guide bar. Check that the sharp part of the cutters on the chain face the tip of the bar.

**8 Align the chain.** Pull the chain around the tip of the bar. This should align the chain with the slot along the bottom of the bar.

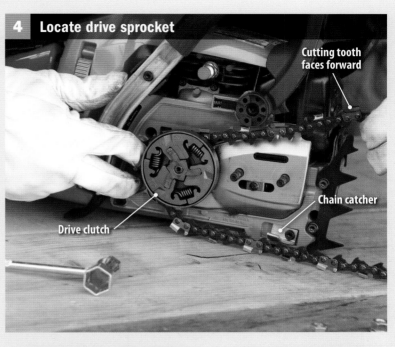

**4** Locate drive sprocket

Cutting tooth faces forward

Chain catcher

Drive clutch

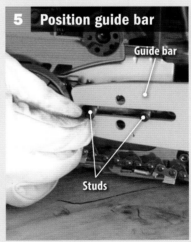

**5** Position guide bar

Guide bar

Studs

**6** Slide guide bar

**7** Place chain links

Chain drive links

**8** Align the chain

# Tension Chain

**1** Align tensioning pin

Align tensioning pin
in matching hole

Adjustment stud
in cover plate

## ADJUST TENSION/ TIGHTEN BOLTS

**1 Align tensioning pin.** Place the bar flush against the saw so the tensioning pin is in the matching hole. On some saws, the adjusting screw and tensioning pin are the same. If the pin is not turned back far enough, it will not protrude through the bar. On other saws, the adjustment stud is in the cover plate (see inset photo). Adjust it slightly so it aligns with the adjustment hole in the bar in order to replace the cover plate.

**2 Replace cover plate.** Replace the cover plate and the bar mount lug nuts. For now, just hand-tighten the nuts. The saw bar should now be flush against the saw motor and the cover plate snug against the bar. Be sure there is no visible gap between these three parts. If there is a gap, the tensioning pin probably is not in its hole in the bar.

**2** Replace cover plate

Drive link

Hand tighten
lug nuts

Tie strap

Cutter

# Tension Chain (continued)

**3 Lift the bar nose.** Pull up on the nose of the bar to lift it into sawing position and keep it up as you tension the chain. If you have a bar with the tensioning system built in (known as an Intenz bar), it is not necessary to hold the bar up while tensioning.

**4 Making adjustments.** Turn the tension adjustment screw (usually clockwise) until the drive links disappear into the bar slot and the bottoms of the chain's lowest tie straps and cutters come up and just touch the bottom of the bar rail (see photo 3). If your chainsaw has a sprocket nose bar, tighten the adjusting screw one-quarter turn more.

**5 Tighten bar mounts.** While still holding the bar nose up, tighten the bar mount nuts with your wrench. Start with the rear nut, then tighten the front nut.

**6 Test chain tension.** To test the chain tension, pull the chain forward several times from engine to bar tip along the top of the bar. The chain should feel snug but still move freely with no binding. As you use the saw, the chain will stretch and you will need to re-tension it. To do this, turn the saw off and leave the "stop" switch in the off position. Loosen the lug nuts about one full turn and follow the instructions from "3 Lift the bar nose" onward.

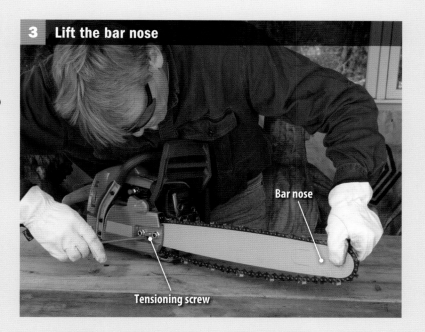

**3** Lift the bar nose

Bar nose

Tensioning screw

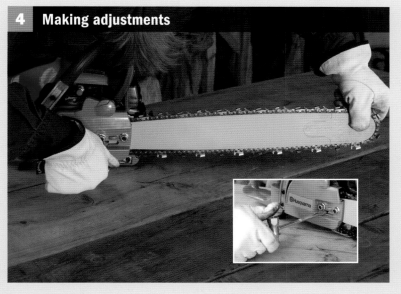

**4** Making adjustments

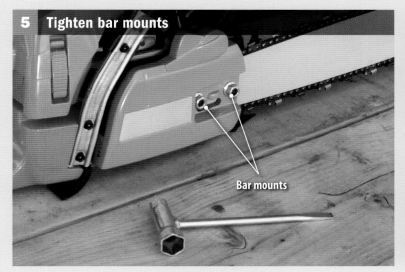

**5** Tighten bar mounts

Bar mounts

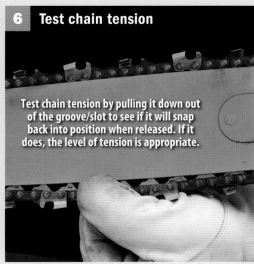

**6** Test chain tension

Test chain tension by pulling it down out of the groove/slot to see if it will snap back into position when released. If it does, the level of tension is appropriate.

# Fuel, Oil, and Lubricants

Gas-powered chainsaws have two-stroke engines, as opposed to the four-stroke engine on most automobiles. On a two-stroke engine, the beginning of the compression stroke and end of the power stroke perform the intake and exhaust functions. Two-stroke engines provide high specific power and are perfect for portable lightweight applications such as chainsaws. But to work properly, they need two-stroke (sometimes called two-cycle) oil mixed with the fuel.

Oil for two-stroke (two-cycle) engines is available in convenient small bottles. Check that the oil is approved for chainsaws.

## FUEL

Start with the gasoline. Your owner's manual should specify the minimum octane level. Most saws need at least eighty-seven or eighty-nine octane gas, which is commonly available as "regular" at most gas stations. The manual also should specify if ethanol or gasohol is acceptable for use and the recommended maximum level blend. Most saws will accept up to a ten percent ethanol to gas blend, standard at the pump in many regions.

## TWO-STROKE ENGINE OIL

Before we go any farther, I want to make one thing clear: There are **two** types of oil used in chainsaws. One lubricates the chain and bar (referred to as bar and chain oil, see page 60). The second, two-stroke (two-cycle) engine oil, mixes with the gasoline to lubricate the engine. The two oils are **not** interchangeable and must not be confused.

Two-stroke engines require a simple lubrication system and the simplest is to mix the oil right in with the fuel. The oil will then reach all of the moving parts of the engine.

On a two-stroke engine, there is no need for an oil reservoir that would depend upon gravity to function properly. That means the engines can be used in any orientation, and that is essential for chainsaws.

Two-stroke engine oil can be petroleum-based or synthetic. Be sure to look for one that is clearly marked two-cycle or two-stroke mix oil. It is also sometimes called premix oil. Not all two-cycle oils are approved for chainsaws, so carefully check the label. Oil is conveniently sold in small bottles to mix with a specific amount of gas, see above. The manufacturer of your chainsaw might even carry its own line of two-stroke mix oil.

Refer to your owner's manual for the manufacturer's recommended gas-to-oil ratio. Failure to mix gas and oil in the correct ratios may cause serious damage to your engine.

**Too much oil in the mixture can cause:**

- Oiling up and fouling of the spark plug
- Loss of engine power
- Carbon deposits on the cylinder, piston, and exhaust
- Excess fumes and smoke from the exhaust

**Too little oil in the mixture can cause:**

- Severe overheating
- Possible engine seizure or failure

The gas-to-oil ratio is not standard in all chainsaws and has changed over time. Years ago, new saws required a 32:1 gas-to-oil ratio (that is, one ounce of oil for every quart of gas). However, that is not so today as many new saws recommend a 40:1 or 50:1 mix. Some synthetic oils on the market guarantee they will lubricate and protect your engine when mixed at 100:1 ratio. This would seem to cut down the amount of smoke and emissions from the exhaust, fouled spark plugs, and carbon build-up.

I have used AMSOIL Saber 100:1 Professional Synthetic Pre-Mix Oil (*www.Amsoil.com*), and mixed it in an 80:1 ratio with absolutely no problems whatsoever. It costs a little more but you use less oil than a 50:1 mix.

## MIXING GAS AND OIL

Oil is heavier than gas and an ounce of oil simply poured in a quart of gas will gently flow down through the gas and sit on the bottom of the can without ever really mixing. In cold temperatures, the oil may also separate from the gas. If the fuel and oil are not mixed well, you will likely have too little oil in the fuel and damage your engine.

Here are the steps I recommend when mixing the gas and the two-stroke (two-cycle) oil:

- Use an approved fuel container and, for safety, remove it from your car or truck and place it on the ground when filling.
- Fill the container with half the gas you intend on mixing.
- Next, add the full amount of two-stroke (two-cycle) engine oil you intend on mixing.

- Replace the cap on your fuel container tightly and shake the container thoroughly to mix the fuel and oil.
- Release the cap slowly, and then add the second half of the gas.
- Replace the cap and shake it well again. (Shake the container, thoroughly again, every time, before refueling your chainsaw.)
- Mark the gas/oil mixed container clearly so you do not confuse it in the future with a container of plain gasoline.

## STABILIZERS

Today's oxygenated gasoline has a relatively short shelf life. For best results, the gas you mix should be used within two or three months. If you do not use your mixed fuel quickly it can deteriorate, leaving engine deposits and gum in the carburetor.

Fuel stabilizers are designed to significantly lengthen the shelf life of gasoline, see photo at right. Some two-stroke (two-cycle) oils such as Husqvarna XP Professional Performance Two-Cycle Oil (*www.Husqvarna.com*) are available with fuel stabilizer already added to them. You may also add a fuel stabilizer such as STA-BIL (*www.GoldEagle.com*) to your gas/oil mix. Always mix it according to the manufacturer's directions at the same time you are adding the engine oil to the gas.

Fuel stabilizers can be added to a pre-mixed gasoline to extend shelf life.

The most convenient (and expensive) way to buy fuel is in pre-mixed cans. The pre-mixed fuel includes a stabilizer.

## PRE-MIXED FUELS

The ultimate in convenience are the pre-mixed fuels that are relatively new on the market (see photo above). Sold in childproof, screw-top, quart-size cans, they include high-octane gasoline, pre-mixed with synthetic two-stroke (two-cycle) engine oil, **and** a fuel stabilizer. Examples include 50FUEL and 40FUEL, which come in a 50:1 mix and a 40:1 mix, respectively, and advertised simply "We mixed it. You pour it." (*www.50fuel.com*). Though expensive, pre-mixed fuel has a two-year shelf life and saves you the hassle of running to the gas station and having gas cans clutter up your garage. You can find it sold as individual quarts or six packs at home centers, hardware stores, and big-box discount stores.

## BAR AND CHAIN OIL

The rivets and links of the chain and the guide bar on a chainsaw need constant lubrication. This is achieved with a bar and chain oil pumped into the top slot of the guide bar by way of the oil pump. Do not confuse this sticky oil with the engine oil added to the gasoline.

Nearly all saws have an automatic lubrication system designed to use one tank of oil per one tank of fuel. Generally, you will need about half as much bar oil as fuel. By design, the oil tank is about half the size of the fuel tank. So, it is necessary to fill up both before resuming saw operations.

Refer to your owner's manual for the recommended oil. Many saw manufacturers have their own brand (see photo below left). SAE #30 weight motor oil is commonly recommended, but the choice may vary based on temperature. Winter grade oil has a lower viscosity to enable it to flow easier in very cold climates. If winter grade oil is not available but needed, you can mix standard oil with ten to twenty-five percent diesel fuel or kerosene (not gasoline because that would damage the saw's oil system components).

Besides petroleum-based oils, there are synthetic oils available. Biodegradable, plant-based oils such as vegetable, nut, and seed oils have also slipped into the market as environmentally friendly alternatives.

Bar and chain oil is available in quarts and gallons at most hardware and home improvement centers as well as chainsaw dealers.

# Fill Oil Reservoir

**1** **Locate oil cover**

Bar oil indicator

**2** **Lay saw down**

**1 Locate oil cover.** Once you have the correct bar and chain oil, identify which cap covers the oil reservoir. On this chainsaw, the oil cap is dark gray and is clearly marked by the manufacturer. It is usually smaller than the fuel cap.

**2 Lay saw down.** Lay the saw on the ground, workbench, or tailgate with the oil cap facing up. Use a brush to clean any dirt or wood dust from around the filler cap before removing it. This will ensure debris does not fall into the tank, contaminate the oil, and block the oil filter.

**3 Remove the cap.** Loosen and remove the oil cap using a combination wrench, screwdriver, or by hand.

**4 Add the proper oil type.** Fill the oil tank with the appropriate bar and chain oil, but do not fill completely. Leave a little room for expansion as the saw heats up. Replace the cap securely and make sure it is tight.

**3** **Remove the cap**

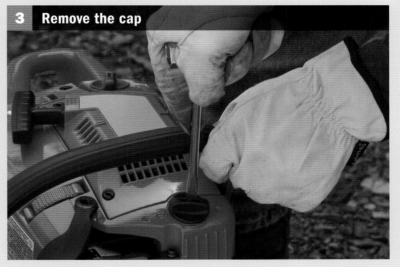

**4** **Add the proper oil type**

# Fill Fuel Tank

**1  Find fuel tank**

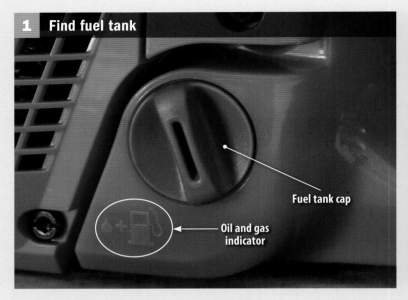

Fuel tank cap

Oil and gas
indicator

**2  Lay saw down**

**3  Remove fuel cap**

## FILL FUEL TANK

**1 Find fuel tank.** Once you have mixed the fuel and engine oil to the correct ratio (see pages 58–59), identify which cap covers the fuel tank. Here the oil cap is green and is clearly marked by the manufacturer.

**2 Lay saw down.** Lay the saw down on flat, stable ground with the fuel cap facing up. Clean any dirt or wood dust from around the filler cap before removing it to ensure debris does not fall into the tank, contaminate the fuel, and block the fuel filter.

**3 Remove fuel cap.** Remove the fuel cap slowly with a scrench, screwdriver, or by hand.

> ### ⚠ WARNING
>
> Liquid gasoline and gasoline vapor are highly flammable and you must keep gasoline away from any source of ignition.
>
> - No smoking anywhere nearby.
> - Store and transport gasoline in approved containers only.
> - Put the gasoline container on the ground for filling. Do not fill with the container on the truck tailgate or in the car trunk.
> - Use a flexible spout you can insert in the saw's fuel tank for filling. Do not spill gasoline on the hot saw. The muffler and spark arrestor may be hot enough to ignite it.

# Fill Fuel Tank *(continued)*

**4** | **Add gasoline**

**5** | **Grease sprocket nose**

**4 Add gasoline.** Shake the fuel/oil mix can and then fill the tank using an automatic fuel stop spout, a flexible spout, or a funnel. Do not fill completely to allow a little room for expansion. Replace the fuel tank cap and tighten securely. Always fill the oil tank with every fill of the gas tank.

**5 Grease sprocket nose.** If your nose has a sprocket, you may want to grease the sprocket nose of the bar. (For more about the advantages and disadvantages of greasing, see Chapter 6 page 174.)

## PRE-START CHECK LIST

❑ **Look for damage, cracks, fuel, or oil leaks**

❑ **Saw body should be clean of dirt, debris, and oil**

❑ **All nuts, bolts, screws, and caps are secure and tight**

❑ **Air filter is clean**

❑ **Brush off debris around carburetor**

❑ **Throttle trigger interlock is working properly**

❑ **Chain catcher is in place and in good condition**

❑ **Chain is tensioned and sharp**

❑ **All personal safety gear is in place**

❑ **All fuel and fueling area is twelve feet away**

❑ **Start on a level surface free of branches, rocks, and other debris**

# Starting the Chainsaw

**1** Activate chain brake

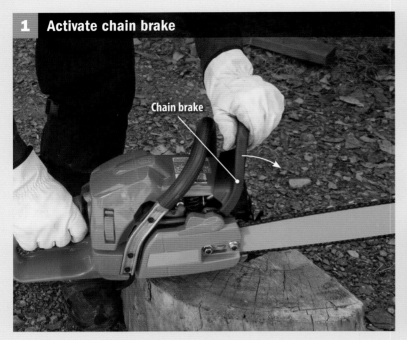

Chain brake

**2** Locate engine switch

**3** Turn choke on

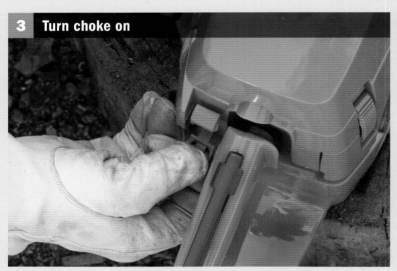

**4** Pump primer bulb

**1 Activate chain brake.** Before starting the engine, grab the top handle guard/chain brake lever and activate the brake by pushing forward on the lever. On a running saw, test the brake as shown in Step 4, page 67.

## SET IGNITION TO "ON" POSITION

**2 Locate engine switch.** Locate the ignition switch (usually near the back handle within your thumb's reach) and set it to the "ON" position.

## SET CHOKE

**3 Turn choke on.** Choke levers, high idle throttle positions, and "ON/OFF" switches vary greatly between manufacturers. Some have all-in-one levers that perform three functions while some have separate controls. Check your owner's manual for their recommended procedure. For a cold chainsaw that has not been run recently, set the choke lever or knob to the closed position. Don't choke a warm engine.

**4 Pump primer bulb.** If your saw has a primer bulb, now would be the time to pump it until you see fuel inside it.

# Starting the Chainsaw *(continued)*

**5** Press decompression switch

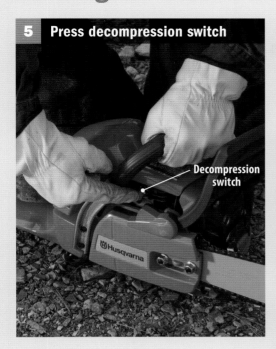

Decompression switch

**6** Stabilize the chainsaw

**7** Kneel for stability

## SET DECOMPRESSION SWITCH

**5 Press decompression switch.** If your saw has a decompression switch, press it. The decompression switch releases the cylinder pressure to ease pulling the starter handle. If your saw has a throttle latch separate from the choke lever (most do not), set the latch to the "ON" position to provide fuel for start up.

## PLACE BOOT THROUGH HANDLE

**6 Stabilize the chainsaw.** To immobilize the rear of the saw, place your right foot through the handle. If your toe does not fit, place the heel of your right foot on the chain guard on the right side of the handle (inset photo).

## KNEEL ON LEFT KNEE

**7 Kneel for stability.** For stability and a straighter back position, kneel on your left knee. (You can stand if conditions are not suitable for kneeling.) Now wrap your left hand around the top handle and hold the saw down firmly.

# Starting the Chainsaw (continued)

**8** Pull

## PULL STARTER CORD

**8 Pull.** Grasp the starter handle with your right hand and pull it out slowly (a few inches) until you feel a slight resistance (the compression stroke). Give a fast pull from this point. Note—do not let go of the starter handle, but allow the rope to recoil slowly. Repeat this step until the engine starts to fire. You will hear a popping sound that indicates the fuel has reached the cylinder and the engine is ready to run.

## MOVE CHOKE LEVER TO OFF

**9 Turn choke off.** Once the engine starts to fire, move the choke lever to the off position and reset the decompression button (if your saw has one). Repeat the starter handle pulling procedure until the saw starts and continues to run. When the saw starts, give the throttle trigger a brief but full squeeze. This will accelerate the saw and return it to the idle position.

## Flooding the Engine

The most common mistake made while attempting to start a chainsaw is flooding the engine. This occurs when the choke is left on too long or the primer bulb is pushed too many times. After you hear the first pop, set the choke to the "off" position. Two or three more pulls should start the saw. If not, you can reset the choke to "on," but as soon as you hear another pop, set the choke to "off" again.

If the engine does become flooded, it will need time for the excess fuel to evaporate or it will continue to be flooded. I usually wait at least five minutes. One way to speed this up is to turn off the ignition, choke, and throttle trigger and pull the starter handle eight to ten times. You could also remove the spark plug to dry it off.

**9** Turn choke off

Choke lever

# Stand Up and Deactivate the Chain Brake

**1 Release the brake.** Stand up with the saw securely held in both hands. Then use your left hand to pull back on the top handle guard/chain brake to release the brake. Pull the far left side of the guard so your hand remains clear of the chain.

## TURN OFF SAW AND RE-CHECK CHAIN TENSION

**2 Tension check.** After running the saw at full throttle for about five seconds, turn it off and re-check the chain tension. Check a new chain's tension every five or ten minutes until it no longer needs tensioning.

## BEFORE CUTTING: CHECK OIL SYSTEM

**3 Oil system check.** With the saw running, test the oiler to ensure proper lubrication to the guide bar and chain. To do this, position the bar above a light-colored surface and rev the engine a few seconds and look for a line of spattered oil thrown from the chain. This indicates a properly working system. If you don't see any oil, clean and check the oil system components.

## BEFORE CUTTING: CHECK CHAIN BRAKE

**4 Chain brake check.** To test the chain brake, hold the running saw about waist level with your left hand firmly wrapped on the top handle directly behind the chain brake. Now accelerate the engine slightly and with your left hand still firmly holding the top handle, rotate your left wrist forward, pushing the chain brake guard until it clicks on and activates. It should stop the chain immediately. If it does not, do not use the saw until you have repaired the brake.

**1 Release the brake**

Chain brake

**2 Tension check**

Check and recheck chain tension

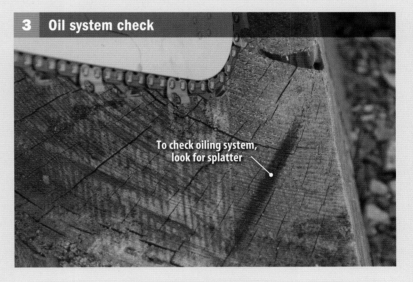

**3 Oil system check**

To check oiling system, look for splatter

**4 Chain brake check**

Push chain brake

## Optional Starting Method: Standing Position

There is another starting method that differs only by the way you hold the saw. This method is done in a standing position without the saw on the ground. Instead of holding the rear handle down with your right foot, lock the rear handle down between your legs at the lower thigh and squeeze gently to immobilize the saw (see photo below left).

Grasp the starter handle with your right hand and pull using the same method as when working on the ground (see photo below right). Once the engine starts, let it idle and remove the saw from between your legs and grasp the rear handle with your right hand.

**Preparing for standing start**

Hold the handle between your legs.

**Proper standing start method**

Standing starts can be handled safely if you follow these instructions

Pull starter handle with right hand.

## ⚠ WARNING

Never drop start (sometimes called throw start) your saw. A drop start is a starting method where the operator holds only one handle while pulling and the starter handle with the other hand. It is unstable because you are contacting the saw at only two points and one of them is a rope. There is no way to immobilize the saw. This is truly dangerous, and has led to many injuries. Don't ever do it.

Do not hold the saw when starting with just your left hand.

Do not hold the saw when starting with just your right hand.

# CHAPTER 5

# Projects

The first commercially available chainsaws were heavy, two-man behemoths associated with burly loggers dressed in red plaid, cutting down giant redwoods. With forty-eight inch and longer bars and weighing more than a hundred pounds, they were not the kind of tool the typical homeowner would be using in his backyard. That all changed after World War II when companies such as McCulloch, Husqvarna, and Stihl saw the opportunity to sell smaller saws, which were still powerful, to a mass market. The weight and relative cost of chainsaws was cut dramatically due mainly to the use of plastics and lightweight alloys. At the same time, improvements were being made in the areas of safety, comfort, and noise level. By 1961, McCulloch ran its first advertisement on network television and chainsaws were now within the grasp of the average homeowner.

Having access to smaller and lighter chainsaws is one thing. Being able to use them safely is another. The purpose of this chapter is to walk through a series of twelve projects that a homeowner with a chainsaw is likely to encounter.

Once you learn to safely use your chainsaw, you can use it to attack a multitude of projects in your backyard, from felling a small tree to trimming brush. This chapter details how to safely handle twelve common projects.

# Cutting Firewood (Bucking)

Make top cuts.

Make undercuts.

Cut the log free.

Cut the whole log.

Perhaps the most common use of a chainsaw for the homeowner is cutting firewood. This is a crosscutting operation and is often referred to as "bucking." It usually starts with a long trunk lying on the ground with most of the limbs or branches already removed. (See Project 8 on pages 126–133 for more about limbing.)

The temptation is to mark the lengths you want your firewood logs and then just cut straight down through the trunk until the piece falls away. That is one of the worst things you can do! Because the trunk is usually lying directly on the ground, you will run your chain right into the dirt. I would much rather cut through a nail and dull two or three teeth than run my saw into the ground and dull all of the teeth on the chain. One errant earth kerf, and it is amazing how everything changes.

You will start pushing the saw harder into the wood to make the teeth cut. The chain and guide bar will overheat. The saw's engine and clutch will also be under excess stress (as will the operator). All of this will lead to operator fatigue—and injury.

Chains become dull just from normal use without digging them into the dirt. Before you start cutting firewood, take a few minutes to sharpen your chain (see pages 187–191).

Tree trunks can be heavy. If they are small enough to pick up, one solution to getting them off the ground is to build and use a sawbuck (see Project 2 on pages 84–91).

Cutting a tree trunk into firewood lengths (called "bucking") requires special techniques to prevent kickback and binding.

# Cutting Firewood (Bucking)

**1** Propping up a large log

Small branches underneath a larger log keep the chain from touching the ground during cutting

**2** Cut projecting limbs

**3** Your saw should self-feed

**4** Cut down from the top

## LOGS ON THE GROUND

**1 Propping up a large log.** Sometimes you can get a larger log up on top of some smaller branches. Then the chain will not touch the ground.

**2 Cut projecting limbs.** At other times, you will be cutting a small piece of wood that is off the ground because it is a part of a larger log. With smaller diameter wood, I simply cut in a downward motion through the wood. I start at full throttle. The reactive force of the chain in the wood will tend to pull the saw toward the wood. Do not apply so much downward pressure that it lowers the engine speed too much. It will cut much faster at a higher RPM.

**3 Your saw should self-feed.** The saw should self-feed, meaning the chain's cutting teeth are sharp enough to bite into the wood without you having to apply much pressure. If you are working too hard, your chain probably needs to be sharpened.

**4 Cut down from the top.** If a long, heavy trunk is lying flat on the ground as this one is, I start by cutting down from the top of the trunk at each point I want to cut through. The straight piece of metal with orange rubber tip on the top of this saw is a Centurion Kickback Guard. For more information, see page 26.

# Cutting Firewood (Bucking) (continued)

### 5 | Stop cutting two-thirds through

### 6 | Repeat at firewood lengths

**5 Stop cutting two-thirds through.** I stop when I am about two-thirds of the way through the cut.

**6 Repeat at firewood lengths.** I repeat this cut down the entire length of the trunk, marking off the lengths of my firewood logs. Note that I am working from the uphill side—any logs that roll, won't roll into me.

## Bucking a tree flat on the ground

- Make the first cut straight down, halfway through the trunk.

- Withdraw the guide bar from the trunk, turn the saw off, and tap a wedge into the top of the cut to keep the chain from binding.

- Restart the engine and without pressing the throttle, slide the guide bar back into the cut. Then continue cutting downward, taking care to stop before the guide bar hits the ground. The log should break apart. If not, kick the log sharply to sever it.

- For a slender trunk, make a top cut between halfway and two-thirds through the trunk, then roll the trunk over and cut down again to meet the first cut.

# Cutting Firewood (Bucking) *(continued)*

**7** **Roll the log**

**8** **Lever with cant hook**

## Dragging a log with a come-along

Wrap a heavy duty chain with a hook around the log, about two feet from the end, using the hook to hold the chain in place.

Fasten a second chain, without a hook, around the trunk of a tree in the direction you want to pull the log. Unless you will be cutting down this tree, protect the bark with a sleeve, such as a bicycle inner tube.

Hook the extendable cable of a come-along to the chain on the log, and hook the stationary end to the chain around the tree.

Draw the log toward the tree by moving the handle on the come-along back and forth.

Release the tension mechanism on the come-along, remove the chain from the tree, attach it to another tree further along, and repeat the process as many times as necessary to move the log.

**9** **Stop rolling halfway over.**

Kerfs facing ground

**7 Roll the log.** Now the trunk needs to be rolled over. A cant hook is a great tool to do this. It has a wooden handle with a pivoting hook at one end that wraps around a log or tree trunk.

**8 Lever with cant hook.** With the leverage provided by the long handle, it is easy to roll the tree trunk away from you.

**9 Stop rolling halfway over.** Stop when the trunk has rolled over one-half turn and the kerfs you have already cut face the ground.

# Cutting Firewood (Bucking) *(continued)*

**10 Complete the cuts.** Cut down from the top to complete the previous cuts. This will keep your saw well above ground level, where it will not be in danger of digging into the dirt and hopelessly dulling the chain.

**11 Completed pieces fall away.** As you finish each top cut, a log will fall away. Move it if it is in your way.

**12 Repeat to complete the task.** Now I will continue until I have cut all of the logs to length.

**10** Complete the cuts

**11** Completed pieces fall away

**12** Repeat to complete the task

# Cutting Firewood (Bucking) *(continued)*

**1** **Use a timberjack**

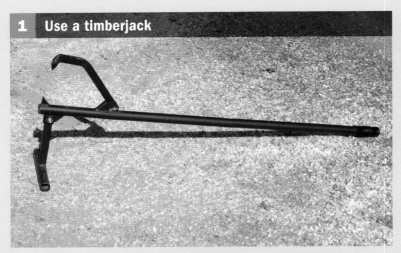

**2** **Hook the log**

**3** **Lift the log end**

**4** **Timberjack props log up**

## USING A TIMBERJACK

**1 Use a timberjack.** There is another way to safely cut logs without digging your chain into the dirt—or even rolling the log over between cuts! It is to use a tool called a timberjack. It is similar to a cant hook, but allows you to raise the log off the ground so you can cut from the top or the bottom.

**2 Hook the log.** First, I catch the timberjack's levered hook under one side of the log.

**3 Lift the log end.** Then I start to lever it over toward me.

**4 Timberjack props log up.** Once the log is completely rolled over, it will be propped up on the timberjack.

# Cutting Firewood (Bucking) *(continued)*

**5** Cut projecting log ends

**6** Pieces fall after cutting

**5 Cut projecting log ends.** On most trees, you can cleanly sever firewood lengths by cutting straight down. The jacked-up log keeps the saw chain safely above the dirt.

**6 Pieces fall after cutting.** Pieces fall after cutting. As I complete each cut, the log falls away. Note that I am careful to keep my head and shoulders to the left of the guide bar so any accidental kickback won't cut into me.

**7 Move the timberjack.** Move the timberjack. Once the cuts get to close to the timeberjack, I roll the log back over, repositioning the jack farther down, so I can continue to work.

**8 Carry on to the end.** Carry on to the end. If your log sections rip, tear, or break off before you complete the cut, you'll need to begin with an undercut a third of the way up before making the top cut that severs the wood.

**7** Move the timberjack

**8** Carry on to the end

# Cutting Firewood (Bucking) *(continued)*

## Problem Logs

Unfortunately, sometimes the log you want to cut is not lying flat on the ground. It could be on uneven ground, lying on other wood, overhanging, or supported at both ends. Each of these problems presents a particular challenge. You have to be able to figure out the pressures on the log or trunk you are cutting in order not to bind the saw in a cut or cause a kickback. This can be done with good observation of the log you will be cutting—and proper cutting technique. But if you cannot figure it out, do not take chances—call a professional.

**1** Start with underside cut

**2** Avoid kickback

**3** Finish cutting from top

## OVERHANGING LOG

**1 Start with underside cut.** This overhanging log should have an underside cut made approximately one-third of the way up from the bottom of the log. I perform this cut as if I was cross cutting, but I use the top side of the guide bar. Be aware this will create pushback that can lead to kickback. Use the following steps to help prevent these problems.

**2 Avoid kickback.** With your left arm straight, remember to keep your left hand thumb wrapped and behind the chain brake. Notice how I keep my body close to the log and to the left side of the guide bar in case the saw does kick back. I use full throttle and high chain speed throughout the slow controlled cut. Be sure your guide bar is long enough and your saw head is close enough so you do not contact the wood with the rounded tip of the bar.

**3 Finish cutting from top.** After cutting upward one-third of the way into the wood, I remove the saw and reposition it on top of the wood. Then I make a cut straight down into the first cut.

# Cutting Firewood (Bucking) *(continued)*

**4 When cuts meet, cut length will fall to ground.** As soon as the two cuts meet, the log will drop to the ground. Be careful it does not hit you or roll onto your feet! What if the two cuts don't meet exactly? If your top cut is a little off to one side or the other, don't worry. Continue sawing until the top cut begins to pass the bottom cut. The small section of wood between the two will break away easily. If you miss by a lot, or if there is a knot in the wood, you might have to make the cut again.

## Bumper Spikes

When cutting down on large wood, make use of the bumper spikes by setting them into the log and pivoting the saw on them by pulling up on the back handle to help assist in driving the saw into the wood. After rotating forward enough, draw the spikes out and push the back of the saw down into the wood to set the spikes again. Pivot the saw on the spikes into the wood. Repeat until the cut is complete.

**4 When cuts meet, cut length will fall to ground**

## Sawing a tree trunk into fire-sized logs

**Beginning a bucking cut**

When the log is propped up off the ground, buck it with two cuts. Make the first cut up from the bottom of the log, then cut down to meet it. This way, the saw won't become pinched and trapped in the cut. Begin by resting the saw's engine housing against the trunk, with the guide bar beneath the tree, and pivoting the housing against the tree. Swing the guide bar up to saw through roughly one-third of the thickness of the trunk.

**Finishing the bucking cut**

Rest the ending housing against the tree, with the guide bar across the top of the trunk and in line with the first bucking cut. Using the housing as a pivot, push the guide bar down through the wood to meet the first cut. Repeat the top cut from the opposite side of the trunk if necessary.

Repeat the bucking cuts along the length of the tree, dividing the trunks into stove-length logs. When you have finished, roll each log onto one side and saw off any remaining limbs.

# Cutting Firewood (Bucking) *(continued)*

## Cutting an unsupported section

When the log is supported at both ends and you want to cut in between, you need to prevent cut trunk sections from falling toward the guide bar and pinching it. Make the first cut from the top through one-third of the trunk. Then, cut up from the underside. Be ready to withdraw should either log move toward you.

## LOG SUPPORTED AT BOTH ENDS

**1 Top cut first.** When a log is held up at both ends, I make the top cut first.

**2 Under cut from below.** The second cut uses the top side of the guide bar on the underside of the log. Be prepared for pushback and kickback. Your left arm should be straight, with your left-hand thumb wrapped and behind the chain brake. I always keep the saw head close to the wood and my body to the left of the cut line. Then, I use a full throttle and a high chain speed, but a slow, controlled cut.

**3 The two cuts should meet.** I aim the undercut so it meets the top cut. If it is a little off, the log will still sever.

**4 Be ready: both pieces will fall.** Both pieces of wood will fall once the two cuts meet. Pull the saw out of the way.

**1 Top cut first**

# Cutting Firewood (Bucking) *(continued)*

**2** Under cut from below

**3** The two cuts should meet

**4** Be ready: both pieces will fall

# Making and Using a Sawbuck

Nail an X-shape.

Make another X-shape.

Add rails.

Enjoy your sawbuck.

There are two problems with cutting (bucking) logs when they are lying right on the ground. The first is you can only cut partially through the log and then you have to roll it over to cut the rest of the way through. If you do not, you will be cutting right through the log and into the dirt—the quickest way to dull your chain.

The second problem is my back. It just does not like leaning over repeatedly to cut up logs. It makes me realize I am not as young as I used to be.

There are a couple of solutions to this problem (a cant hook and a timberjack) for large diameter logs (as explained in Project 1, Cutting Firewood (Bucking) on pages 72–83). But even those methods do not get the log up at a comfortable height for cutting.

A better solution for medium- and small-sized logs is to make a sawbuck. There are lots of sawbuck designs, but the simplest is just a pair of *X*-shaped assemblies made out of construction lumber and nailed together with a couple of cross rails. The sawbuck is simply a cradle that holds the log at a comfortable working height. You should be able to make one in less than half an hour from material you might already have in your garage or shop. And it should last for years.

A sawbuck made from construction lumber is a great way to get logs off the ground for convenient, safe bucking into firewood lengths.

# Making and Using a Sawbuck

### 1   Find appropriate lumber

**1 Find appropriate lumber.** I found a couple of 2 x 6s in the shed. Start by cutting four lengths to about four feet each. I am securely holding the pieces in place with my left foot as I saw.

**2 Wood forms *X*-shapes.** Two of the pieces will form one of the *X*-shaped subassemblies. I eyeball the angle and the position of the cross-rails.

**3 Nail boards together.** Five two-and-one-half inch (8d) nails make the connection. Three are driven from one side of the *X* and two from the other side. The angles on the first *X* are not critical.

### 2   Wood forms *X*-shapes

### 3   Nail boards together

## ⚠ CAUTION

Construction lumber is difficult to saw, so to eliminate the risk of kickback I used a small chainsaw with a nose guard to crosscut the lumber for my sawbuck, and I was careful to hold the wood down on the curb with my foot. If you don't have such a chainsaw, I recommend that you crosscut the lumber using some other kind of saw: table saw, portable circular saw, handsaw, miter (chop) saw, or saber saw.

# Making and Using a Sawbuck (continued)

**4 Match angles of *X*'s.** The second *X* should be assembled at the same angle as the first. I lay the third and fourth pieces of 2 x 6 on top of the first *X* and nail them together from one side with three nails.

**5 Nail second subassembly together.** Then I flip the second *X* over and nail it with two more nails.

**6 *X*'s will be three feet apart.** While standing the *X* subassemblies up, I decide they need to be about three feet apart.

**4** Match angles of *X*'s

**5** Nail second subassembly together

**6** *X*'s will be three feet apart

# Making and Using a Sawbuck *(continued)*

**7** Cut two rails

**7 Cut two rails.** Next, I cut two 2 x 6 cross rails to three feet each. The rails will form a cradle to hold small branches and short logs.

**8 Starting the nails for rails.** I find it easiest to start two nails about three-fourths inch from the ends of each cross rail, working right down on the driveway.

**9 Nail rail in place.** Holding the cross rail about three inches from the top of the X, I nail it in place.

## Techniques for safe cutting

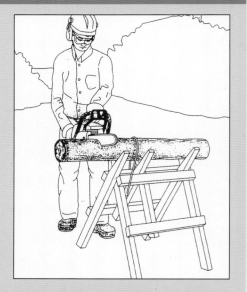

Position yourself to one side of the blade—should the saw kick back or cut through wood more quickly than expected, it will not hit you. When cutting lightweight logs to stove-box length, set them in a sawbuck and attach a hold-down strap to keep the log from moving.

**8** Starting the nails for rails

**9** Nail rail in place

# Making and Using a Sawbuck (continued)

**10  Attach rail to second X**

**11  Second rail forms cradle for log**

**10 Attach rail to second X.** Next, I nail the other end of the first cross rail to the other *X*.

**11 Second rail forms cradle for log.** To form the cradle for the logs, I nail the second cross rail to both *X* subassemblies. Notice it will stick out beyond the *X* on each end so it aligns with the first cross rail.

**12 Toenail the final nails.** To make access for the hammer, I toenailed in the final nails.

**12  Toenail the final nails**

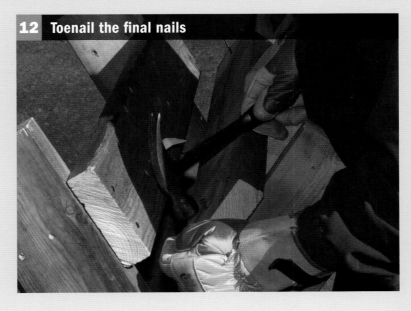

# Making and Using a Sawbuck *(continued)*

**13 Sawbuck completed, but high**

**14 Lowering the sawbuck**

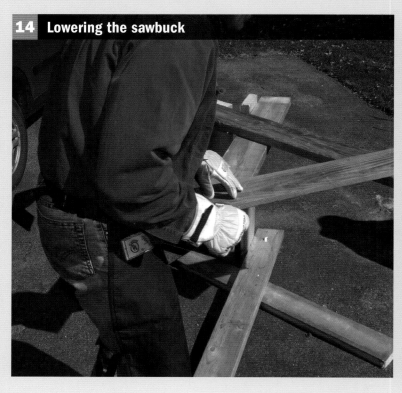

**13 Sawbuck completed, but high.** With it all set up, I notice it is a little bit too high. I want to be able to cut holding the saw just below waist high.

**14 Lowering the sawbuck.** To lower your sawbuck by three inches and at the same time give it flat feet, first I mark a line across both legs with a scrap piece of 2 x 6.

**15 Cut along the lines.** The last step is to cut all four legs on the pencil lines.

**16 Using your sawbuck.** To use the sawbuck, lay the log in the cradle so it sticks out one end a little longer than the final length you want to cut off.

**17 Cut and fall.** Then, cut off the length of firewood you need with your chainsaw and let it fall to the ground.

**18 Continue cutting.** Continue to move the log in the cradle, cutting off as many lengths as possible.

**15 Cut along the lines**

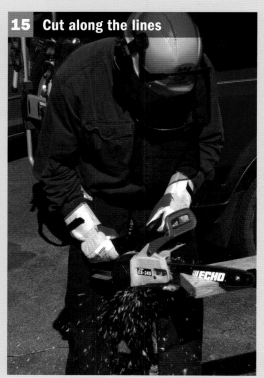

# Making and Using a Sawbuck (continued)

### 16 Using your sawbuck

### 17 Cut and fall

### 18 Continue cutting

⚠ **WARNING**

As the pieces become shorter, do not try to hold the log in the cradle or the piece hanging outside the sawbuck with one hand and cut with the other. Always keep both hands on your chainsaw!

# Splitting and Stacking Firewood

Raise the maul overhead.

A mighty blow.

Accelerate on impact.

Aim for the stump.

**S**ome people consider splitting and stacking firewood an art form. It is not as easy as it looks to split a round log into two halves exactly where you want. There is actually a learning curve to the process. But it is a great feeling when you hit a log just right and it splits right down the center (or in quarters). Now it is time to put away the chainsaw and get out the hand tools. Yes, you can buy or rent a hydraulic or cone-screw splitter (see box on page 96), but it is probably not worth it unless you have many logs to split.

When splitting a log, focus the swing so it goes all the way through to the bottom of the log.

## Starting the wedge

Set up the log, large end up, on a splitting stump that is about one foot high, and wider than it is tall.

Hold a steep splitting wedge against the log between the center and the edge, perpendicular to the wood grain; if there is an open crack radiating from the center of the log, insert the wedge into it. Alternatively, use a twisted wedge, which splits wood more easily and is less likely to become stuck.

With a 6- to 12-pound long-handled sledgehammer, tap the wedge into the wood deep enough for it to stand on its own.

## Driving the wedge

Holding the sledgehammer with both hands, pound the wedge down gradually to split the log. Swing the hammer only as high as you feel comfortable, and do not force the sledge downward—let it fall onto the wedge, allowing gravity to do most of the work. With practice, you will be able to execute a full, overhead swing of the hammer and hit the wedge squarely.

For an especially large or hard-to-split log, repeat the procedure with a second wedge, working in a line across the center of the log until it splits.

For logs up to six inches in diameter, you can try a splitting maul, which is designed to split logs in one blow. It works with straight-grained wood.

To split wood by hand, you can use an ax, a sledgehammer with a wedge, or a wood splitter's maul. For most logs, I prefer a maul—basically a wedge with a handle.

The advantage of a maul over a traditional ax is that the wedge head on the maul (with its more abrupt slope) is less likely to stick in the wood and more likely to increase outward pressure on the wood.

For tough wood, you may have to fall back onto a wedge (or two) with a sledgehammer. And I usually keep a couple of wedges around for gnarly and problem wood.

Mauls come in a variety of sizes—six-, eight-, or ten-pound models. There are also twelve- to fifteen-pound mega or monster mauls available (check with *www.Baileysonline.com* or *www.LogSplitters-IronOak.com*). The advantage of a lighter maul is it can be swung faster. And, surprisingly, velocity is more important than mass in producing good results when splitting. With a mega maul, you often can split a log with one blow, but it takes a while to learn how to swing that much weight effectively.

A splitting maul has a wedge-shaped head and a strong handle.

With wood splitting, size and strength are not as important as technique. Here are some things to consider when you first start splitting wood:

- **The longer the log**, the more difficult it will be to split. If you are a beginner, start out learning your technique with short logs (twelve inches or shorter). On the other hand, after you have had some experience, start a splitting session with the largest and ugliest logs first, saving the small ones for when you are tired.

- **Study the log**. Look for an existing crack in it and position the crack so it aligns with your swing. Try to avoid splitting through knots or twisted grain.

- **Learn to strike** within a quarter-inch of your desired spot. Practice.

- **Do not try to hit** the exact center of a round log, especially if it is over sixteen inches in diameter. By hitting closer to one edge, the maul strikes the growth rings where they are wide and vulnerable.

- **Never make a half-effort blow** as they seldom split the log and will be discouraging. It is better to take a rest between swings if necessary.

- **You will get significantly more force** if you visualize and aim at the bottom of the log rather than the top. Focus your swing so it goes all the way through the log, not just whacking the top.

- **If you are having trouble** splitting a log, try turning it end for end or spin it ninety degrees.

- **Even before you start** splitting, when you are bucking up logs with your chainsaw, always try to cut the ends of each log as square as possible. It takes a lot more energy when splitting to get a good hit on a sloping surface or a leaning log.

Study the log and spin it for the best cutting position.

A perfect hit! It is right on an existing crack in the log.

## Whittling down a thick log

A log more than 18 inches in diameter may be more difficult to split with one or two blows.

Hold a splitting maul parallel to the wood grain and strike the log four to six inches from its perimeter, splitting a wedge of wood from the log. A wedge and a sledgehammer can be used instead.

Work around the log until the core that remains is small enough to split.

## ⚠ CAUTION

**Safety Rules for Splitting**

- Split logs can fly in lots of directions. Wear good boots and long pants or chaps.
- Set up a twenty-foot radius around wherever you are splitting and keep anybody (including assistants, and especially kids) out of it while you split.
- Teach others to always approach you from the front, never behind.
- Wear good gloves and do not wait too long to replace them—you will pay with blisters.
- As you tire, you will be tempted to put your feet closer together. Avoid this and use it as a sign that it might be time to quit for the day.

## Using a cone-screw splitter

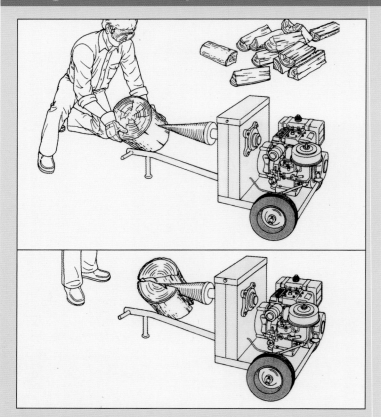

Hold the side of a two- to four-foot long log diagonally against the point of the revolving cone, resting the log on the support bar (top). As soon as the cone has seized the log, let go. The threaded point of the cone will draw the log toward the cone's wider base, causing the wood to split in half (bottom). Remove the log halves and split them into quarter sections, if desired, by pushing the split face of each of the halves against the cone.

■ **Set up your log** on a firm, flat surface. If you set up on soft ground, all you end up doing is spending energy pushing the log into the ground. If you are in the woods, a stump might work as long as it is not too high. A solid gravel driveway works fine as does a short thick log on end.

■ **Be aware that all woods** split differently. Good, straight dry oak is a breeze where locust or elm can be very difficult. Some wood splits easier when green while others (such as the pines) split easier when dry.

■ **Sometimes the most tiring thing** is not the splitting, but the constant switching from swinging to setup after each split. If I am doing a lot, I will set up about ten to fifteen logs in a row (it looks like a cemetery). Then I split through them all right down the line. Next, I will walk through the mess and set it up again, then split again, continuing this process until everything is small enough to burn.

■ **Your back will last longer** if you split for thirty minutes, then move and stack logs for thirty minutes, etc.

## Using a hydraulic splitter

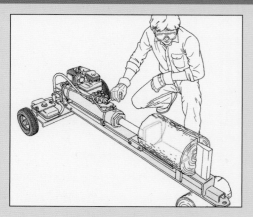

Level the bed of the splitter by propping the lower end on a solid base, such as a split log. Then, set a log up to four feet long on the bed, butting one end against the hydraulic ram. Steady the log with one hand, push down the lever, and let go of the log. The ram will drive the wood against the wedge.

To split a half-log into quarters, lay the split face against the bed and activate the ram as before.

# Splitting and Stacking Firewood

**1 Measure swing distance**

**2 Hold maul horizontally**

**1 Measure swing distance.** I start by placing the cutting edge of the maul right where I want to strike the log. It is almost like aiming a rifle. This also helps me measure the distance from where I will be standing when I strike the log. From here, I step back about a third of a step so I will lean forward a little to add power as I complete the swing.

**2 Hold maul horizontally.** Next, I hold the maul horizontally near waist level, elbows comfortably bent with one hand at the base of the handle and the other next to the head.

**3 Raise maul overhead**

**3 Raise maul overhead.** Flexing my knees slightly, I abruptly raise the maul overhead, extend my arms, and rise up on my toes to gain maximum energy. My right hand slides down the handle to meet my left hand.

**4 Make downward swing forceful**

**4 Make downward swing forceful.** With a forceful downward swing, I bend at my waist and my knees to get my whole body into the action. Notice the marching stance and the long reach. I find this the best way to give momentum to the maul's head and power it into the wood with authority.

# Splitting and Stacking Firewood *(continued)*

**5 Accelerate the maul on impact**

**6 Concentrate on follow through**

**7 Finish with knees crouched**

**5 Accelerate the maul on impact.** When the maul head hits the wood, I continue to power it downward by lowering my shoulders and hands, and snapping my wrists downward.

**6 Concentrate on follow through.** The wood splits apart as I concentrate on follow through and where I want the blow to finish—the bottom of the log.

**7 Finish with knees crouched.** Note my final position: I am crouching with my knees bent slightly. My hands—and the maul's handle—end up low enough that a mis-strike would drive into the ground, not into my feet or legs.

# Splitting and Stacking Firewood (continued)

## Stacking and Seasoning Firewood

The best wood for burning has been seasoned (dried). Green, freshly cut wood has a moisture content of about sixty percent. It will smolder when lit, produce a good deal of smoke, and little flame. Much of the fire's heat is wasted evaporating the water. Burning unseasoned wood will also cause a rapid buildup of creosote in the flue of your fireplace or stove and increase the risk of a chimney fire.

Split logs usually should be seasoned to about twenty percent moisture content by drying them for six to twelve months. Wood cut, split, and stacked properly in early spring should be ready by fall.

Wet wood should be stacked in a sunny spot that is exposed to the wind, well away from the house, and supported off the ground as shown

in the drawing below. This allows air to circulate around the wood to prevent rot, and discourages termites and other wood-eating insects from crawling into the woodpile, or worse, into your house.

Here is a stacking tip: Mix the sizes (large, small) as you stack because you will need kindling and large logs to build a fire. This method also helps fill the crevices, creating a steadier pile.

Once the logs look dark and withered, and their ends have cracks that radiate from the center, they are probably seasoned. One way to test for dryness is to tap a couple of logs together. Dry logs make a sharp, ringing sound; you will hear a dull thud if the wood is green. Once the wood is dry, cover the stack with a tarp to shed rain and snow.

One other thing: If you want to know how much your firewood (and all your hard labor) is worth, you can measure the pile and compare it to the current prices you see listed in your area. Firewood is usually sold by the cord or partial cord (sometimes called a face cord or rick). When comparing prices, be sure to find out if it is seasoned and what type of wood it is (Hardwood? Softwood? Species? Lengths? Split?).

One full cord equals a stack that is eight feet long, four feet high, and four feet deep (128 cubic feet of stacked firewood).

One partial cord, a face cord or rick, equals a stack that is eight feet long, four feet high, and anywhere from one to three feet deep (so the logs will fit in your fireplace or stove).

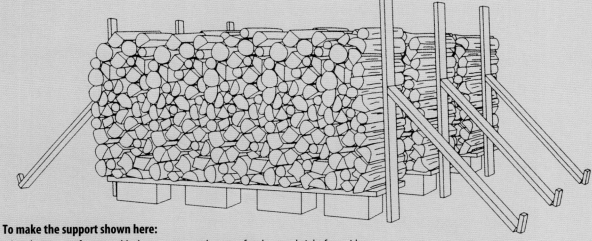

**To make the support shown here:**

- Lay three rows of concrete blocks over an area about ten feet long and eight feet wide.
- Set an eight-foot pressure-treated 2 x 10 on each row of blocks.
- Drive a pressure-treated 2 x 4 support 1 foot into the ground at each end of the 2 x 10s.
- Brace the supports with diagonal 2 x 4s beveled at the top end. Fasten the diagonal boards at the top with galvanized common nails. At ground level, hold them in place with 2 x 2 stakes.
- Pile the logs on the 2 x 10s with at least twelve inches between rows to allow air to circulate.
- The stack can be covered on top with a sheet of plastic, held down with logs.

# PROJECT 4

# Trimming Overhead Branches

Loppers are safe.

Bow saw severs branches.

A pole saw reaches high.

Powered pole saw.

O ne thing I feel strongly about is not using a chainsaw when cutting overhead. It is too easy for a branch to come crashing down onto me, bringing the running saw with it. In such situations, I recommend switching to a lopper, bow saw, or pole saw, or else calling in a professional.

Loppers are like a giant pair of scissors or garden pruners, but with long handles to get extra leverage. A good sharp pair of loppers can cut through branches up to two-inches thick.

A bow saw (sometimes called a bucksaw) is a handsaw with a large C-shaped tubular handle and a thin steel blade with large aggressive teeth. It can cut through branches of just about any thickness, but will quickly cut through limbs up to about four inches.

Finally, there are a couple of kinds of pole saws. A manual pole saw has snap-together handle segments with a sharp steel blade at the end and often a lopper blade (controlled by a cord pull) on the back of the saw. Power pole saws are small gas- or electric-powered chainsaws on the end of extension poles.

A manual pole saw allows you to reach high overhead to trim dead branches from a tree.

# Trimming Overhead Branches

**1  Loppers handle overhead work**

**2  Getting into tight spots**

**1 Loppers handle overhead work.**
Loppers are perfect for trimming overhead errant branches, as on this ornamental crabapple tree. But be careful; branches can still fall on your head.

**2 Getting into tight spots.** It is easy to fit a pair of loppers into a tight spot that might be difficult to safely reach with a chainsaw. Even if you could get the chainsaw in there, the flexible branches would not cut easily and would tend to throw the saw around dangerously.

**3 Bow saw works well.** These overhead limbs are easy to remove and clear out some working space while the tree is still standing. For safety, I used a bow saw to cut them off instead of a chainsaw.

**4 Using a manual pole saw.** Dead and unwanted branches high up in a tree can be reached with a manually operated pole saw. Here, I am able to cut a dead branch straight down. Though the teeth are sharp, cutting from this distance can give you a workout. Note that I am wearing a helmet!

**3  Bow saw works well**

**4  Using a manual pole saw**

# Trimming Overhead Branches (continued)

**5 Cutting live branches.** On a live branch, I make a cut with the pole saw in three steps. First, I make a small undercut so my final cut does not strip the bark. Then, I make a top cut a little farther out to drop the branch. And, finally, I cut down to remove the stub.

**6 Using powered pole saws.** Gas- and electric-powered pole saws normally reach eight to fourteen feet in length. They are very unwieldy because the weight of the saw is way out there on the end of a heavy pole, and so are the forces exerted by cutting with the moving chain. That's why powered pole saws are professional tools best left to professional arborists. Because the saw itself is some distance from the user, the big risk is that cut branches fall upon the operator. The tool's unwieldiness also poses the risk of inadvertently cutting any objects within reach of the extended pole—including power and telephone lines. Having read these cautions, if you insist upon using one, pay attention to these points:

- Keep bystanders far away.

- Follow all chainsaw operating rules, and wear complete personal protection equipment, including helmet and jacket with Kevlar-reinforced shoulder yoke.

- Since you'll be looking up at the work, pay special attention to your footing and stable stance, and clear away any obstacles with tripping potential.

- Don't power up the saw until you are in position and ready to cut.

- Don't cut a branch that is directly above you, lest it fall on you.

**5 Cutting live branches**

**6 Using powered pole saws**

# PROJECT 5

# Trimming a Hedge

Mount comb device.

Start high, sweep down.

Trim shrubs.

Fell saplings.

It does not take long for a hedge to get out of control. If not trimmed regularly, it can grow so thick and high that you will need to climb onto a ladder to trim it. The usual power tool to trim a hedge is a hedge trimmer. They come in gas-, electric-, and battery-powered models.

You might think the chainsaw is a good alternative. The problem is, the moving chain deflects thin branches instead of cutting them. Trying to cut anything that can move is dangerous because the moving object also can move the saw, most likely to where you don't want it to go. Trimming a hedge with a regular chainsaw is dangerous and should not be attempted. Fortunately, an inexpensive attachment for the saw bar makes the job possible. It looks like a giant comb with a tip guard and is called the Clip-N-Trim. It is available for about $20 from Granberg International (*www.Granberg.com*).

The comb device weighs less than one-and-one-half pounds and will fit twelve-, fourteen-, sixteen-, and twenty-inch chainsaw bars. The fixed prongs on the attachment stop small branches from moving while the chain does the cutting. In addition to trimming hedges, you can use it for a couple of other operations not normally recommended for the standard chainsaw—cutting heavy brush and pruning small trees.

By adding an inexpensive comb attachment, a chainsaw can be used as a hedge trimmer.

# Trimming a Hedge

**1** Mount comb device

**2** Rake across face of hedge

**3** Giving a bush a hair cut

**1 Mount comb device.** Start by mounting the comb-like Clip-N-Trim attachment to the right side of the chainsaw bar using the bar bolts and a mounting bolt at the nose of the bar. You may notice I'm not wearing my helmet or face shield. That's because this hedge has no large branches that might hit me.

**2 Rake across face of hedge.** Here I give a haircut to a large burning bush by raking the attachment across the face of the hedge.

**3 Giving a bush a hair cut.** Though it will cut on the top or the bottom of the bar, I find it easiest to cut a straight line by starting with the bar almost vertical.

# Trimming a Hedge (continued)

**4** | Finishing the hair cut

**5** | Attacking thorny/thick growths

**6** | Handling saplings

**4 Finishing the hair cut.** Then I lower the bar across the branches until the bar is horizontal.

**5 Attacking thorny/thick growths.** The comb attachment makes quick work of trimming thorny and thick growth such as this ornamental crabapple tree.

**6 Handling saplings.** Most of the saplings on the side of this hill could be cut with the hedge-clipping attachment.

## PROJECT 6

# Felling a Small Tree

Saw the notch.

Make back (felling) cut.

Keep your body stable.

Remove saw, observe fall, escape safely.

There is nothing simple about felling most trees. Perhaps I would consider a small tree, with a slight lean, in the middle of a field, on a windless day, simple. Anything else can be anything but simple.

Due to the surprising weight of a tree and the power it possesses, the forces it can exert are tremendous. A careless mistake or miscalculation could destroy property, or earn you a trip to the hospital or worse. If you are not confident in your ability to handle the saw or properly assess the situation and do the job safely, you should leave it to a professional.

One of the worst scenarios is to leave a half-fallen tree—one that gets hung up in a tree or trees around it. It is like a stick of dynamite where the fuse burns right up to the stick: too dangerous to approach and too dangerous to leave alone. If this happens, do not try to be a hero. Clear the area of bystanders until a professional tree service can remedy the situation.

Once the tree is down, it must then be limbed (see Project 8 on pages 126–133) and cut up, or bucked (Project 1 on pages 72–83), which require a completely different set of skills.

Finally, you must plan any tree fall safely and, as my father always told me, "Keep your mind on what you are doing!"

Jen Ruth makes an angled cut to join the horizontal cut and complete a notched scarf.

Notched Scarf:
An angled cut joins
a horizontal cut

# Felling Plan

Before you tackle the tree, it's important to make a felling plan. This simply means looking and thinking methodically to figure out:

- where the tree would most naturally fall,
- where you would prefer it to fall,
- what you can do to direct its fall,
- where you will go while it falls,
- what clearing and other preparations you need to do first.

## DIRECTION OF FALL

It is usually easy to decide the direction you would like a tree to fall, but getting it there can be a different story. You have to assess the risk of having the tree fall the wrong way and what damage it could cause. If there are buildings, power lines, or other trees around, perhaps you should have a professional take down the tree. A large tree can literally cut a house in half. (For more on felling a tree near a building, see Project 9 on pages 134–147.)

The following things will influence the direction of fall:

- **Natural Lean.** It can be difficult to fell a tree in a desired direction if it is leaning in an opposite direction.
- **Weight Distribution.** If the tree's crown (branches and upper weight) puts more weight on one side of a tree than the other, the tree will tend to fall in the direction of its heaviest side. Snow and ice can also influence weight distribution.
- **Entanglement.** A tree that is naturally entwined with another tree or connected to another tree by way of a climbing vine can be difficult to fell, and it is almost impossible to assess which direction it will fall.
- **Defects.** If the tree is anything but solid and healthy, safe felling could be

Using an ax as a plumb bob, it is easy to see that this tree has very little lean.

difficult. Rot, punky wood, or a hollow trunk may not be visible from the outside of the tree. Look for external scars, dead wood in the crown, or ants and other insects. Tap the trunk with your ax and listen for a hollow sound. This is almost a sure sign of extensive heart rot and the tree should be avoided or left to a professional to fell.

- **Wind.** The force wind can exert on a tree may greatly affect its fall direction. Take a look at the strength and direction the wind is blowing. If you are trying to fell the tree against the prevailing wind, you likely will lose.

To tell which way a tree is leaning, hold your ax between your thumb and forefinger at the end of the handle as gently as you can. Now with the ax head down, use the ax as a plumb bob. You'll be able to see which way the tree is leaning. The tree in the photo above, though growing on a slope, is straight up and down.

## ESCAPE ROUTE

Before felling any tree, it is a good idea to think through your escape route. Most felling accidents happen within twelve feet of the tree stump. If a tree snaps off its hinge during a fall, it usually kicks back over the stump. Also, if the tree you are felling is on a hill, it is more likely to kick back over the stump as well as slide or roll down the hill until it comes to rest.

In addition, as the trunk falls, it is likely to bounce off its branches, and this could send it in any direction—including back toward the stump or to either side of the stump.

So, the first question is, what is the normal direction you would move out of the way as the tree falls? And then, what if the tree does not fall in the normal direction?

The best plan is to clear an escape route diagonally away from the direction of fall.

This usually means some cleaning out of brush from around the tree so you have good footing and to prevent your saw from inadvertently hitting a branch or stick.

Also, clear out any deadwood, live trees, or saplings from the direction of fall to prevent them from being thrown back during the fall.

If the tree you are cutting has branches below shoulder height, cut and remove these from the working area and escape route as well. And look up in the tree for widow makers—dead branches that may become dislodged and fall on you. Remove them if you can; be very wary of them if you cannot.

Finally, clear out bystanders. I always recommend a safe distance of at least two times the height of the tree for people and property.

For safety, always clear short trees and brush from the working area, the area where the tree will fall, and your escape route.

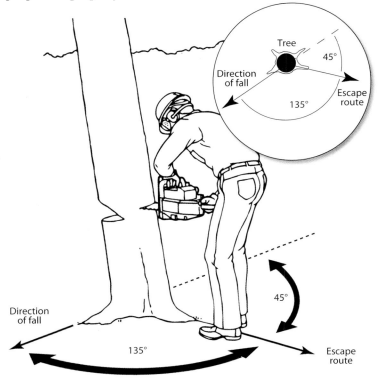

**Plan your escape route.** When the tree begins to fall, turn off the chainsaw and retreat to safety along an escape route. The best route is along a line 135° back from the direction of the tree's lean.

## MAKING FELLING CUTS

With the individual tree's situation considered and a felling plan in place, it is time to start cuts. There are two basic cuts you need to know about: the scarf (or notch) cut and the back (or felling) cut.

They are placed in such a way as to create a hinge of wood that helps determine the direction of fall. The scarf cut creates an opening so the hinge can direct the tree's line of fall. Not only does the hinge hold and control the tree during its fall, but it also breaks itself in two toward the end of the fall.

There are several types of scarf cuts, but for the photos here, Jen will use the most common: the standard scarf. This scarf cut consists of two precise cuts. When complete it looks like a wedge cut out of the tree trunk, facing the desired direction of fall.

### Two basic cuts: scarf and felling

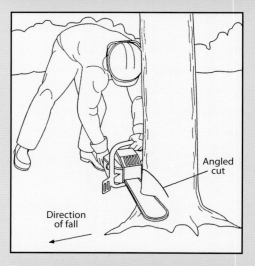

**1. Cutting a scarf (notch).** On the side of the tree that faces the direction of its natural lean, hold a chainsaw with the blade angled at forty-five degrees to the trunk. Turn on the engine, let it come to full throttle, and make an angled cut about one-third of the way through the trunk. Pull the blade from the cut. Holding the blade horizontally at the bottom of the angled cut, saw into the end of the angled cut (left). Retract the blade and push the wedge-shaped piece from the notch.

**2. Making the felling (back) cut.** On the side of the trunk opposite the notch, start a horizontal cut two inches above the bottom of the notch (right). Stop cutting when the blade is two to three inches from the back of the notch, creating a hinge (below). The width of the hinge should be about ten percent of the trunk diameter. The trunk will pivot on the hinge, and the tree should fall. If not, drive in wedges.

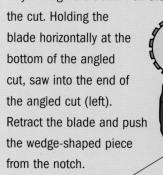

# Felling a Small Tree

**1 Making the horizontal scarf cut.** This tree leans slightly toward the desired direction of fall. There's no wind, so good felling cuts should do the trick. The first (or lower) cut of the scarf should be level and horizontal. Jen stands on the side of the tree so the direction of fall will be directly to her right. With her knees slightly bent, she holds the saw about waist high, with the left side of the front handle in her left hand. (Your left hand will not be behind the hand guard/chain brake; therefore, it is important to have cleared any brush from around the tree to help avoid kickback.) With the engine housing resting against the tree, she brings the engine to full throttle and drives the guide bar into the tree, swinging in a horizontal arc. She cuts between one-quarter and one-third of the way through the diameter of the tree. Then, she will reduce the engine to half throttle, remove the saw bar from the cut, and the throttle down completely.

**2 Making the angled scarf cut.** The second (or top) cut is a little more difficult. It should start above your first cut and angle down to meet your first cut. The goal is to precisely meet your first cut at its deepest point. For softwoods, the angle of cut should be forty-five degrees. For hardwoods, it should be thirty degrees. Loggers differ on the most sensible order of cuts when making the notch. Many believe it is easier to line up the two cuts cleanly if you make the upper sloping cut first, then make the horizontal cut to meet it (as shown at left).

**1 Making the horizontal scarf cut**

The horizontal scarf cut is level

**2 Making the angled scarf cut**

The angled scarf cut meets the lower cut at its deepest point

# Felling a Small Tree (continued)

**3** Keep guide bar square

Hold guide bar even along its diagonal path

**3 Keep guide bar square.** When making the second cut, Jen pushes the guide bar squarely along its diagonal path, not in an arc as she did before. I like to stop about one-third of the way through, remove the saw, and check my progress from both sides of the tree. If the kerf is not aligning with the first cut, I readjust my saw angle and start cutting again.

**4 Remove the wedge of wood.** A chunk of wood that resembles a triangular slice of watermelon will be removed when both cuts meet one-third to one-quarter of the way into the tree.

**5 The felling cut.** Next, make a felling cut horizontal and level like the first scarf cut but on the opposite side of the tree and one to two inches higher than the horizontal (bottom) scarf cut. This cut is also called the back cut because it is made opposite the direction of fall. Jen holds the saw with her left hand on the side of the front handle. She bends her knees slightly and positions her feet for good stability. Before cutting, look back over your shoulder—to the right is your escape route.

**4** Remove the wedge of wood

Remove the wedge of wood created by the two scarf cuts

**5** The felling cut

The felling cut should be one to two inches higher than the scarf cut

1 to 2 inches

# Felling a Small Tree (continued)

**6 Hinge wood.** Throttle up and make the cut, but stop before you reach the scarf cut. This allows for a strip of wood to act as a hinge. Because Jen is felling the tree in the direction of its natural lean, the hinge wood should be uniformly wide from one side of the tree to the other, and its width should be one-tenth of the diameter of the tree (a ten-inch diameter tree should have a one-inch hinge and a twenty-inch diameter tree should have a two-inch hinge).

**7 Pullers can start pulling.** As the back cut nears ten percent of hinge wood, your rope pullers (if you are using them) should start pulling. Or the tree may start to pivot on the hinge on its own and start to fall. Or the tree may lean back the wrong way on its hinge. You need those rope pullers, and you may need to drive wedges into the saw cut to redirect it (see page 116).

**8 Remove. Observe. Escape.** As soon as the tree starts to fall, Jen removes her saw and observes the direction it is falling. If it's falling correctly and you have a clear path toward your escape route, as Jen does, shut off your saw, set it down (or, as shown here, engage your chain brake and take it with you), and retreat along your escape route.

**6  Hinge wood**

Keeping your body stable, with your feet planted firmly while cutting, will help ensure your safety

**7  Pullers can start pulling**

Know when it's time for your pullers to do their job

**8  Remove. Observe. Escape.**

Escape route

Fall line

## ⚠ WARNING

If your saw gets stuck in the cut and the tree is falling, abandon it. Let go and escape. You probably will not be able to pull it out and you are risking injury staying close to the tree as it falls.

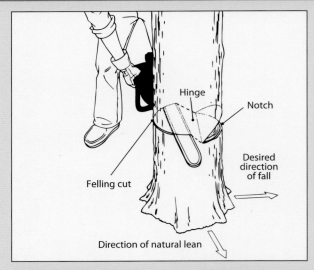

**Cutting an angled hinge.** To make a tree fall in a direction perpendicular to its natural lean, cut a notch on the side of the tree facing the desired direction of the fall. Then, opposite the notch, make a horizontal felling cut at an angle so that one end is closer to the back of the notch than the other, creating a hinge with ends of unequal width. The wider end of the hinge should be opposite the direction of the natural lean.

**Driving wedges to fell the tree.** Just next to the narrow end of the hinge, drive two aluminum or plastic wedges into the felling cut. The wedges will shift the tree's center of gravity away from the natural direction of the lean, forcing the tree to fall in the direction of the notch. If the tree does not fall, remove the wedge closest to the hinge by hitting it from the side with the sledge hammer. Deepen the felling cut slightly, then drive the wedge back into the cut.

**A Barber Chair** occurs when a tree splits lengthwise up the trunk as it is being cut, presenting a significant danger to the chainsaw user.

## BARBER CHAIR

When a tree is leaning or being wind blown, it may have a tendency to do something called a barber chair—when a tree splits lengthwise up the trunk as it is being cut. As the top of the tree falls, it springs a slab of tree trunk backward, opposite the line of fall. For this reason you must never stand directly behind a tree, opposite the line of fall while back cutting.

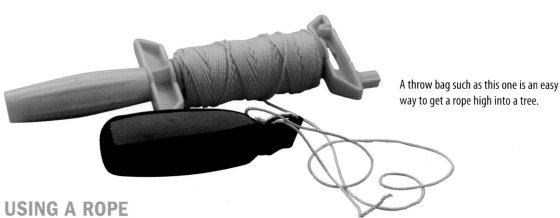

A throw bag such as this one is an easy way to get a rope high into a tree.

## USING A ROPE

A rope can help direct the line of fall. The rope should be three-eighths inch or one-half inch in diameter, but more importantly, of ample length. The length of the rope should be at least twice the height of the tree.

For the best leverage, it is best to tie the rope two thirds of the way up the tree. How do you get the rope up that high? I like to use a throw bag. It is a heavy bag filled with shot attached to a lightweight nylon line. After you throw the bag over a large branch or crotch in the tree, you can use the line to pull a heavy rope into position.

As the chainsaw will be running when it is time to pull the rope, before any felling cuts are made, the sawyer should work out a procedure to signal the puller or pullers when to pull. I have always used an exaggerated head nodding so I can keep both hands on the saw.

### ⚠ WARNING

Do not tie a rope to a vehicle and try to pull a tree away from its natural lean. The rope is likely to snap when the tree decides to go the way of nature and not the vehicle's way. And too much pulling pressure too early can lead to a barber chair.

## Guiding a falling tree with block and tackle

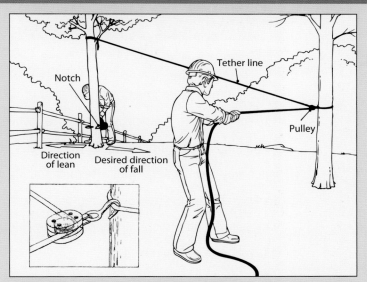

**Attaching a tether line and pulley.** Tie one end of a one-inch manila-rope tether line around the tree to be felled; fasten the line with a square knot as high on the trunk as you can reach. Run the line to a tree situated roughly in line with the desired direction of fall, and fasten a pulley assembly (inset) to its trunk, about two feet from the ground. Pass the tether line through the pulley and have a helper pull the line taut at a ninety degree angle. Make sure your helper is standing well away from the line of fall, at a distance at least twice the height of the tree being felled.

Cut a notch in line with the desired direction of fall and, as you are making the horizontal felling cut on the opposite side of the trunk, have your helper pull on the tether line to control the direction of the fall.

# Felling a Large Tree with Wedges

Saw the notch.

Start the felling cut.

Drive wedges.

The tree falls.

I am a firm believer in and staunch user of, felling wedges. To me, they are inexpensive insurance, especially when felling larger trees or ones where you are just not quite sure which way it will naturally fall. There is nothing worse than thinking you have a tree all figured out. You did not even put a rope in it, and three-quarters of the way through the back cut, your saw gets pinched.

Somehow you misread the tree and it started leaning the wrong way, closing on the back cut and pinching the bar and chain. Perhaps you misread the lean, the crown weight, or the wind. It does not matter how it happened, because above your head, hanging by a thread, you have several tons of wood that is liable to fall in any direction at any time.

For a few dollars, this situation could easily be remedied with one of man's oldest tools—the wedge. Felling wedges, which are manufactured in steel, aluminum, and plastic, have much less taper than those used for splitting wood. The wedge is driven with an ax or sledgehammer into the back cut. A wedge provides a mechanical advantage that causes the tree to lean toward the intended line of fall.

Wedges driven into the cut help determine the direction a large tree will fall.

Nose of saw bar

Wedges

## Make a Felling Plan

This big old pine stands in the path of the new driveway, so it has to come down. My first step is to make a felling plan. I can't take any chances with this one, because if it falls the wrong way it could smash my new house (this photo was shot from a third-floor window).

- The best direction of fall is straight down the old driveway. There's nothing in the way to obstruct the fall.

- I'm going to use felling wedges driven with an ax to help ensure the tree falls where I need it to go.

- The tree doesn't lean, there's no wind, the crown is centered, and no nearby trees can hang it up, so I don't think I will need pullers on a heavy rope.

- I'm certain the power lines are on the other side of the house, so there's no risk they'll become involved.

- My escape route has to be back and to the left. There's nothing in my way.

Wedges made from steel are usually reserved for professionals felling large trees, and for wood splitting. If you hit a steel wedge with your chainsaw, it almost guarantees you are going to have to sharpen or change your chain. For that reason, I would recommend avoiding steel felling wedges.

Plastic wedges are light, inexpensive, and will not damage your chain but can chip and break when being driven and can pop out of the cut if you strike too hard. My choice is aluminum wedges. They are lighter than steel, and if hit accidentally, will not dull your chain like steel. They are also less prone to damage from driving with an ax or sledgehammer than plastic wedges.

Use felling wedges on trees that are at least twelve inches in diameter. In addition to the wedges, you will also need a strong sledgehammer or ax to drive them in. The process of using wedges to fell a tree starts out just like felling a smaller tree (see Project 6, pages 108–117).

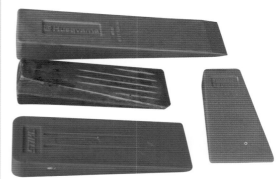

Plastic or aluminum wedges are recommended for most jobs when felling trees.

# Felling a Large Tree with Wedges

**1 Making first cut.** Start with the lower (horizontal) scarf cut, cutting on the side you want the tree to fall. It is made horizontally about waist high and at full throttle. I cut about one-quarter to one-third of the way through the trunk and then throttle down and back the bar out of the cut.

**2 Making second cut.** Next, I make the top scarf cut down at an angle of about forty-five degrees (for softwoods) or thirty degrees (for hardwoods). The goal of this cut is to meet the lower horizontal scarf cut, at its deepest point.

**3 Remove wedge of wood.** A wedge-shaped piece should fall away, leaving the completed scarf cut facing the desired direction of fall. If the scarf cuts do not meet precisely, trim them until they do before making the back cut; but be sure you don't cut any deeper than one-third of the tree's diameter.

**4 Making the felling cut.** The felling cut is made on the other side of the tree. It is a horizontal cut about one to two inches higher than the first scarf cut. I stop cutting once the kerf is just deep enough for a felling wedge to be driven in so it is snug. Never cut all the way to the scarf cut.

**1 Making first cut**

Lower scarf cut

**2 Making second cut**

Top scarf cuts down at 45° angle

**3 Remove wedge of wood**

**4 Making the felling cut**

Horizontal back cut on opposite side of tree

# Felling a Large Tree with Wedges (continued)

**5** **Turn saw off**

Because it is turned off, the saw can remain in kerf or be removed while wedges are being driven in

**6** **Drive wedges into back cut**

Back cut

Wedges

**7** **Cut deeper with chainsaw**

Stop cutting as holding wood approaches about two inches

**5 Turn saw off.** I turn off the saw, set the manual brake, and leave it in the trunk while I drive the wedges. (You can remove the saw from the kerf if you prefer.)

**6 Drive wedges into back cut.** Drive the wedges into the back cut with an ax or sledgehammer. I usually use at least two wedges. Here, I have driven an aluminum wedge in the center and two plastic wedges on either side of it. Note the chainsaw head coming out of the left side of the trunk and the tip of the guide bar coming out of the right side. Before you start to cut, make sure the wedges aren't contacting the saw chain.

**7 Cut deeper with chainsaw.** With the wedges in place, I start up the chainsaw and cut a little deeper. I stop cutting once the back cut approaches about two inches of holding wood (the hinge).

## Driving wedges

At the narrow end of the hinge, drive two aluminum or plastic wedges into the felling cut.

If the tree does not fall, drive in larger wedges.

Wedges also can help release a stuck saw by bearing the weight of the tree that has settled back on the chain; but avoid touching the chain with the wedge.

# Felling a Large Tree with Wedges (continued)

**8** Drive wedges further into cut

### 8 Drive wedges further into cut.
I tap the wedges in a little deeper with my ax.

> ⚠️ **CAUTION**
>
> Be patient and take your time going back and forth between cutting a little and tapping the wedges a little. Do not try to make the tree fall until it is ready to do so.

### 9 Cut deeper, drive wedges deeper.
Because the tree still has not fallen, I cut another half-inch of hinge wood and drive the wedges deeper. The wedges are actually lifting one side of the tree and causing it to lean in the direction you intend it to fall. Depending on the size of the tree, the wedges may require substantial pounding. With the tree still standing, I cut one more half-inch from the hinge, leaving at least ten percent of the trunk diameter of holding wood (hinge) from one side of the tree to the other. I know I am getting close now, so I extract the saw and drive the wedges one last time.

**9** Cut deeper, drive wedges deeper

Remove another half-inch from the holding wood

# Felling a Large Tree with Wedges *(continued)*

## 10 Fall begins; follow your escape route

Wedges dislodge and fall as the tree begins to fall

**10 Fall begins; follow your escape route.** The tree should start to fall, so now it is time to take my pre-determined escape route diagonally away from the line of fall. Some of the wedges are falling to the ground.

**11 A perfect, safe fall.** This was a perfect fall, exactly where I wanted the trunk to fall.

## 11 A perfect, safe fall

Tree falls exactly where planned by following procedures outlined

## Cutting a wide notch for a large tree

Position the chainsaw horizontally as for the second part of a notch cut. Make the first cut by rotating the guide bar into the tree for a distance equal to one third of its diameter. Then make a diagonal cut to meet the horizontal cut. Moving across the tree and working from the other side, make a companion pair of cuts, lining them up with the first pair to create a large notch across the entire face of the tree. Knock out the wedge-shaped piece of wood.

# Felling a Large Tree with Wedges (continued)

**12 Note the appearance of different cuts.** After the tree falls, you can see the different parts of the cut in the stump. On the near side is the lower scarf cut. Behind that in the middle is the rough remains of the hinge. And the back cut is on the far side.

**13 Ready for limbing.** The fallen tree is now ready for the next procedure, limbing (see Project 8 pages 126–133).

**12 Note the appearance of different cuts**

Back cut

Remnants of hinge

Lower scarf cut

> ⚠ **WARNING**
>
> Cutting a tree whose diameter is greater than the length of your saw's bar is extremely dangerous. Cutting with the bar nose can result in a kickback and must be done with caution—and should not be attempted by novice sawyers.

**13 Ready for limbing**

## PROJECT 8

# Limbing a Downed Tree

Beware of kickback.

Keep trunk between body and saw.

Saw limbs to firewood length.

Always safety first.

So, you felled a tree or came across one that is already down on the ground. What do you do now?

Sectioning a downed tree can be risky business because of stress and pressure on the limbs and branches. The weight of the tree is pushing down on trapped branches and bending them. And, if you plan on cutting up the tree for firewood, the branches will just get in your way. The first step is to remove the exposed limbs and branches. The process is called "limbing."

Trees that are partially uprooted, but not completely downed, create special problems and hazards. For these, you should call in a professional. No matter what the situation, limbing can be complex, depending on the type of tree you are cutting up and its structure. Because cutting any trunk, log, limb, or branch that can move is difficult and dangerous, you must be extremely careful. Let's start with a few general rules and then work through the process of removing the limbs and branches.

Limbing means using the chainsaw to safely remove all of the exposed branches and limbs.

# Limbing a Downed Tree

**1** Body position is important

Dangerous body position—bending over chainsaw

WRONG!

## ⚠ WARNING

Tree branches and small trees that the tree has landed on and bent over can be under a great amount of stress. These are called spring poles and are aptly named because when you cut them they tend to spring back to their original position. If you are in the path of one of these wooden whips, you can be seriously injured. They can also throw, pinch, or kick back a chainsaw.

Take a few minutes to identify any spring poles among the tree branches so they can be dealt with appropriately. Many times, smaller ones can be trimmed out of your way by hand with loppers or a bow saw. Using a chainsaw to remove spring poles can be risky because the cut can cause the severed end to fly back and kick the saw toward you.

**1 Body position is important.**
When limbing, do not bend over the saw because it would put your upper body in a dangerous position.

**2 Avoid chainsaw kickback.** Be aware of the bar tip's position. Here the upper quadrant of the tip is about to enter the wood, which could lead to kickback.

**2** Avoiding chainsaw kickback

Avoid attempting to cut within the chainsaw's kickback zone (top front of bar)

WRONG!

# Limbing a Downed Tree (continued)

**3 Kickback danger.** When you must stand on the same side of the tree trunk as the limb, change your cutting angle so the bar tip does not contact the tree trunk as you complete the cut.

**4 Best body position while limbing.** This is the safest position for limbing. I am standing on the opposite side of the tree trunk from the branches I am cutting. If the tree is on a hill, stand on the uphill side if possible. This is in case the tree rolls down hill when you remove any supporting branches. When standing on the steep uphill side of a trunk, adjust your stance to keep your legs away from the guide bar.

## Trimming limbs from a trunk

Starting at the top of the tree, hold the guide bar parallel to the trunk, keeping the trunk between you and the saw. Cut toward the bottom of the tree through the base of the limb; do not let the tip of the guide bar hit the ground or any branches.

Cut off all of the limbs on one side, then move to the other side of the trunk and limb the opposite side. Leave the limbs on the underside of the trunk intact, to raise and support the trunk during bucking.

If the tree lies across a slight incline, brace the trunk by leaving several limbs on the downhill side to keep it from rolling. Stand on the uphill side to make the limbing cuts. Adjust your stance to keep your legs away from the guide bar when cutting limbs on the uphill side.

**3 Kickback danger**

Kickback danger zone

WRONG!

Continuing this cut will put the bar nose in danger of contacting the tree trunk and kicking back

**4 Best body position while limbing**

It's safest to stand on the opposite side of branches being cut

# Limbing a Downed Tree (continued)

**5 Body versus kickback zone**

Keep your upper body back away from the chainsaw's kickback zone

Kickback danger zone

**5 Body versus kickback zone.** Stand with your upper body away from the saw's kickback zone. Use a firm and balanced stance. I am not leaning or reaching, but moving my body to position it for each cut. I make a habit of removing those branches that hinder reaching other branches first.

**6 Trim branches from trunk.** Jen is reaching over the trunk to trim off branches parallel with the trunk. For safety, she always tries to keep the trunk between her body and the saw. She progresses along the trunk, cutting off all the limbs on one side, then on the other. She will leave the limbs under the trunk as legs. They are dangerous to remove now and will help support the trunk later during bucking.

**7 Cutting large limbs.** Large limbs are almost the same as small trees and should be removed with two cuts. If they are leaning toward one side of the trunk, I will make a small undercut (one-quarter to one-third of the way through) on that side. This will relieve any compression stress.

**6 Trim branches from trunk**

Keep tree trunk between you and the saw while trimming branches

**7 Cutting large limbs**

Large limbs equal small trees, so follow same safety rules outlined in Project 6

# Limbing a Downed Tree (continued)

**8** **Large limbs require two cuts**

Making a second cut on a large limb

**9** **Keep brush cleared**

Keeping brush and cut limbs cleared from work area provides safety to operator

**8 Large limbs require two cuts.** Then, I will make the second (final) cut down from the top of the limb slightly closer to the tree trunk. This will relieve tension as it frees the limb.

**9 Keep brush cleared.** As you are working, stop often to remove small limbs and brush to allow easier access to the remaining limbs to be cut. Many of these can be easily cut with handheld loppers, a bow saw, or chainsaw loppers (see box on page 133). If cutting with a chainsaw, cut slowly and observe branch motion to avoid pinching the saw. If you can move a branch tip down by pushing down on it (as Jen is doing here), it is not a supporting branch and should fall when cut.

**10 Safely cutting limbs from log.** If limbs are being cut for firewood, it is easier to cut them to length while they are attached to the tree. I trim the branches from the end starting where the limb is still large and strong enough not to move from the pull-in force of the chainsaw. To ensure it doesn't move during the cut, place the saw body against the branch.

**10** **Safely cutting limbs from log**

Select point of limb where it remains strong and the running chainsaw cannot move it

# Limbing a Downed Tree *(continued)*

**11** Continue cuts along limb

**11 Continue cuts along limb.** I am working my way up the trunk, cutting pieces to length to fit my fireplace and stove.

**12 Cut until you reach the trunk.** I will continue cutting lengths off the limbs until I reach the trunk. Then it is time to start bucking (see Project 1 on pages 72–83).

**12** Cut until you reach the trunk

Continue cutting the limb until you hit the trunk, and then switch to bucking

# Limbing a Downed Tree (continued)

## Chainsaw Lopper

A relatively new and surprisingly inexpensive item on the market that works great for many limbing operations is Black & Decker's Alligator Lopper. It has been called a lopper on steroids.

The Alligator Lopper can easily cut through branches up to 4 inches in diameter.

This unusual tool has a six-inch chainsaw incorporated into one side of a large scissors-action lopper. Because guards cover the chainsaw, kickback is less of a worry. The opposite side of the lopper holds the branch in place as the operator squeezes the handles to cut it. The saw is electric powered and designed for safe and quick cutting of branches up to four inches in diameter. It is lightweight, at six-and-one-half pounds, but the 100-foot maximum recommended length extension cord will restrict your mobility (*www. BlackAndDecker.com*).

The Alligator Lopper grabs and cuts in one easy motion.

## Chainsaw Buddy

The chainsaw buddy is another useful attachment for bucking small logs and branches that are on the ground. It consists of an aluminum fork that bolts onto the saw bar, which you can use to lever underneath the wood and hold it in position for clean cutting. With the log held by the buddy, sawn wood falls away on both sides of the bar, avoiding a pinch (*www.ChainsawBuddy.com*).

PROJECT 9

# Felling and Limbing a Tree Near a House

Bow saw is safe overhead.

Scarf (notch) cut.

Wedge the felling cut.

Limb and buck.

Felling a tree in the middle of the woods or a field is one thing, but felling one that is dangerously close to a house or some other object you want to save is a completely different story. If it falls in the wrong direction, or takes the power lines down with it, it could be a catastrophe.

Many years ago when the house shown in these photos was built, the homeowner planted a little two-foot high pine tree as part of a landscaping project. The problem is, it was planted less than three feet from the house. That cute little pine tree grew to become taller than the house with a trunk that was more than twenty inches in diameter at the base! Not to mention that it was leaning.

The challenge was to remove the leaning tree, but to make certain it fell in the right direction—away from the house. In this case, the power lines are underground and not a problem. Once it fell, there was another problem. It is a pine with branches every few inches shooting out in all directions. Getting the tree down was only half the battle. The rest was safely removing all of those branches and maybe getting some firewood out of the trunk and larger branches.

It was time to take down this pine tree that had grown to become a danger to the house.

# Felling a Tree Near a House

**1 Clear the work area**

**2 Consider lean, set fall plan**

## ⚠ WARNING

Whenever you do tree work in a residential area, you are more likely to have spectators. People seem to enjoy watching the activity, often at unsafe distances. Be sure everyone—including pets—is at least two tree lengths away, no matter which way the tree might fall.

Also, residential trees often contain screws, nails, staples, and parts of old fences. The bark just grows over them and hides them. They will be at the exact same height as they were at the time they were driven. Be careful. A nail can damage and even break a saw chain.

## FELLING THE TREE

**1 Clear the work area.** The first step in any chainsaw project is to make sure you have a clear work area. In this case, the downspout has to be removed.

**2 Consider lean, set fall plan.** Next, I take a good look at the tree to see how it was leaning. If it fell naturally, my guess is it would probably come down right alongside the house (and crush the air conditioner). I decide to make the scarf (wedge) cut clearly opposite the house. The tree should fall in the direction of the scarf cut. You must always be certain the tree will clear power lines and neighboring houses.

## ⚠ WARNING

Be sure there are no overhead power lines near the tree you intend to fell. If there are any, don't take chances—you had best call in a professional.

# Felling a Tree Near a House (continued)

## 3 Remove lower limbs

## 4 Don't use chainsaw overhead

**3 Remove lower limbs.** It is best to get some of these big lower limbs out of the way while the tree is standing. It also opens up the work area.

**4 Don't use chainsaw overhead.** It is dangerous to use a chainsaw overhead, so I cut the limbs off close to the trunk by hand with a bow saw. I can safely operate a bow saw with one hand and control the falling branch with the other.

 **WARNING**

Whenever working overhead, use a hand tool (instead of a chainsaw) and wear a helmet.

## Felling a tree away from the lean

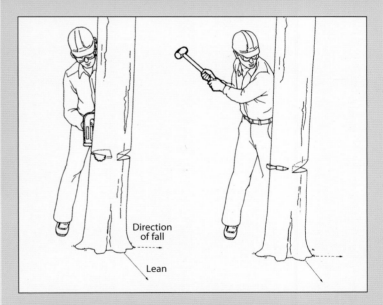

Make the notch cuts on the side where you want the tree to fall and angle the felling cut so the thick part of the hinge is opposite the natural direction of lean (above left).

Drive wedges into the felling cut near the thin side of the hinge (above right). The wedges will force the tree upward on that side (inset), shifting its center of gravity away from the lean. If the wedges do not cause the tree to fall, deepen the felling cut.

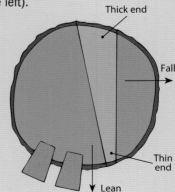

# Felling a Tree Near a House (continued)

**5** | **Make horizontal scarf cut**

Horizontal scarf cut

**6** | **Cut a quarter of the way in**

**7** | **Make angled scarf cut**

**8** | **Scarf cut guides fall direction**

**5 Make horizontal scarf cut.** I make the first scarf cut level and horizontal.

**6 Cut a quarter of the way in.** This level cut should go in about one quarter of the thickness of the tree.

**7 Make angled scarf cut.** Next, I make the second scarf cut down at an angle of about forty-five degrees to meet the first. A wedge of wood falls out and onto the ground.

**8 Scarf cut guides fall direction.** Even though the tree is leaning the other way, this scarf cut will help guarantee it falls away from the house.

# Felling a Tree Near a House *(continued)*

**9** | Make the felling cut

**10** | Wedges open felling cut

**11** | Wedges encourage tree's fall

**12** | Tree not falling yet

**9 Make the felling cut.** Now I make a horizontal felling cut (back cut) on the opposite side of the trunk from the scarf cut. I will leave about twenty percent of the diameter of the tree. This uncut area is called the hinge.

**10 Wedges open felling cut.** To start to open up the felling cut, I pull the saw out of the cut and place an aluminum wedge into the cut.

**11 Wedges encourage tree's fall.** Tapping the wedge with the blunt end of the ax (the poll) drives it in and encourages the tree to fall.

**12 Tree not falling yet.** Hmmm... the wedge is in as far as I can drive it and the tree has moved slightly in the right direction, but it does not seem to be falling yet.

# Felling a Tree Near a House *(continued)*

**13** Make felling cut deeper

**14** Keep additional cuts small

**15** Tree begins to fall

**16** Slow fall takes three seconds

# Felling a Tree Near a House (continued)

### 17 Wedge remains in tree

### 18 Many limbs to be removed

**13 Make felling cut deeper.** I slide the saw back into the kerf ahead of the wedge and cut a little more, making the hinge a little bit smaller. I will drive the wedge farther into the cut.

**14 Keep additional cuts small.** You can bring the saw back into the kerf from either side of the tree. Make small cuts, tapping the wedge between cuts.

**15 Tree begins to fall.** One last good whack with the ax and the tree starts to fall—away from the house.

**16 Slow fall takes three seconds.** Though it took ten minutes from when I started making the first scarf cut to this point, it only took three seconds from the point where it started to fall until it was completely down on the ground. Your retreat must be quick.

**17 Wedge remains in tree.** With the tree down right where I wanted it to fall, you can see that the wedge cut into the hinge—and it is still there.

**18 Now the real work begins.** This pine tree has many limbs to remove and cut up.

## Felling a sharply leaning tree

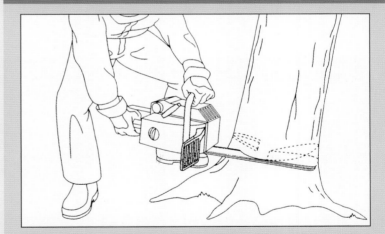

As shown in the inset, a series of cuts may be necessary to fell a tree that leans sharply. First, make shallow cuts on each side of the trunk parallel to the direction of fall to prevent the tree from splitting behind the notch cut.

At the same level as the side cuts—but perpendicular to them—cut a notch halfway into the trunk.

Finally, make the felling cut.

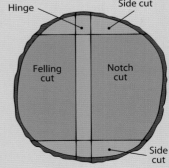

# Limbing and Bucking a Tree Near a House

**1 Start bucking at base**

**1 Start bucking at base.** I start bucking logs off the clear section from the base of the trunk. First, I make a cut up from the bottom of the trunk about one quarter of the thickness.

**2 Finish cut from top.** Then, I cut down from the top until the log falls off.

**3 Think before cutting limbs.** I have now come up to the point where there are limbs, and this takes some studying. First, I will start by clearing off some of the limbs on the top of the trunk. They are not under any pressure.

## ⚠ WARNING

Wherever possible, always stand on the uphill side of the trunk when bucking off logs. That way the logs will not fall or roll onto your legs or feet. Wear steel-toed shoes. And notice the stable "marching stance" I take when cutting.

**2 Finish cut from top**

**3 Think before cutting limbs**

# Limbing and Bucking a Tree Near a House (continued)

**4** Sprung limbs are dangerous

**5** Start with small notch

**6** Finish cut from outside

**4 Sprung limbs are dangerous.** The weight of the tree rests on this sprung limb. The limb is dangerous because there is tension on the outside of the bend in it, and compression on the inside of the bend. If I were to try to cut it through from the inside, the bar would become pinched. Cutting from the tension side, where I am pointing, would cause the branch to split and spring before being completely severed.

**5 Start with small notch.** I start to deal with this sprung limb by making a very small cut (one-quarter of the limb diameter) on the inside of the limb, to relieve some tension and act as a small scarf notch.

**6 Finish cut from outside.** I finish the cut from the outside, being careful to keep the tree trunk between the sprung limb and me. When the limb suddenly breaks free, I do not want to be in its path. Keep a firm grip on the saw, because sprung branches can throw the saw as they spring free.

# Limbing and Bucking a Tree Near a House *(continued)*

**7** Carefully remove limbs

**7 Carefully remove limbs.** Next, I continue to work down the trunk watching for more limbs under pressure. (Notice the sprung limb with pressure released in the foreground.)

**8 Some sprung limbs are okay.** It is okay to leave some of the sprung limbs along the bottom for now, as legs to hold up the trunk. I will cut them off later when the weight of the tree is reduced greatly by removing the rest of the limbs.

**9 Twigs create problems.** Tiny branches and twigs can be troublesome because they move and flex. The temptation is to cut them with the tip of the chainsaw, but that can lead to kickback. It is safer to turn off the saw and use hand loppers to clean these off close to the trunk.

**10 Trunk narrows near the top.** As I get near the top end of the tree, the trunk is getting very thin. Cut it off as if it was a large limb.

**8** Some sprung limbs are okay

# Limbing and Bucking a Tree Near a House (continued)

## ⚠ CAUTION

The safest cut is usually with the trunk between you and the saw. I reach over the trunk if possible. This way, a spring limb won't hit you when you cut it free. For safety, stand on the opposite side of the trunk from the limb you are cutting.

## 9   Twigs create problems

## 10   Trunk narrows near the top

# Limbing and Bucking a Tree Near a House (continued)

## ⚠ CAUTION

One final safety note on this project. Take your time as you work. Occasionally, turn off your saw, set it down, and do a little housecleaning. Clear out the cluttered branches and logs so they do not get in the way. Pile everything neatly. If you are meticulous in your work habits, you are much less likely to have an accident.

**11 Buck the trunk.** I work my way back down the trunk, cutting pieces to firewood length.

**12 Remove final support.** There are only a few limbs supporting the remaining trunk. I notch them each from below and then cut them off from the top so as not to trap the saw bar in a closing cut.

**13 Buck the large limbs.** After the trunk is all cut up, I switch over to cutting some of the limbs into firewood. I used some of the larger logs I cut earlier to support the limbs. I have added a 16-inch length gauge (white plastic rod with a red-tipped end) to help cut the firewood to a consistent length. It is called the Quick Stix Firewood Log Guide and is available to fit most chainsaws (*www.QuickStixMfg.com*).

**11** Buck the trunk

# Limbing and Bucking a Tree Near a House (continued)

**12 Remove final support**

**13 Buck the large limbs**

PROJECT 10

# Cutting Down a Stump

Saw halfway up.

Wedge frees saw bar.

Push log off.

Saw at ground level.

Scarf cuts are rarely made down close to the ground. As explained in Project 1 (pages 108–117), they are made at a comfortable and safe working height. You are usually left with a stump of about three feet high. If it is out in the woods, you can probably just leave it. Eventually, it will decompose. Even if it is in a backyard or garden, you might want to leave it as a decorative item; perhaps mount a birdbath or birdfeeder on top of it. If it is a large stump, you might even tempt a chainsaw sculptor to carve it.

But sometimes, as when I cut down the large pine tree next to the house (see Project 9, pages 134–147), it just has to go. In this situation, the stump was very heavy, so I decided to take it in two steps. First, I cut it down about halfway. Then I cut it down to about three inches from the ground. (See the box on page 153 for some ideas on completely removing it.)

The tree stump disappears when it is cut down to a few inches above the ground.

# Cutting Down a Stump (continued)

**1** Horizontal cut comes first

**2** Cut around stump

**3** Blade pinched

**4** Turn off saw, insert wedge

**1** **Horizontal cut comes first.** Kneeling on one knee, I start by making a horizontal cut about a foot off the ground.

**2** **Cut around stump.** I slowly cut in deeper, working my way around the stump. The tip of the guide bar should never be cutting. That can lead to kickback.

**3** **Blade pinched.** I am about three-fourths of the way through the cut, but the weight of the trunk and tension in the wood has caused the kerf to close on the bar, pinching it in place.

**4** **Turn off saw, insert wedge.** I quickly turn off the saw, which is hidden behind the trunk in this photo, and tap in a plastic wedge.

## ⚠ CAUTION

Use a plastic wedge instead of a steel one when you are trying to free a pinched bar. The plastic wedge will not damage the saw chain, should it come in contact with it.

# Cutting Down a Stump (continued)

**5 Remove pinched chainsaw.** With the wedge in place and the saw off, I can pull out the pinched bar.

**6 Resume stump cutting.** Leaving the wedge in the kerf, I start up the saw again and finish the cut.

**7 Finishing the job.** Then, I push the log off the stump.

**5** Remove pinched chainsaw

**6** Resume stump cutting

**7** Finishing the job

# Cutting Down a Stump (continued)

**8** **Make the final cut**

**8 Make the final cut.** The final cut will be made just about three inches above the ground. Clear any dirt that may be mounded up to avoid dulling your chain.

**9 Follow procedure a second time.** The process is the same but here I am down on both knees. Just be sure to keep the bar horizontal so you do not cut into the ground.

**10 Small, low stump remains.** Finally, the cut is completed and the stump is left only a couple of inches high.

> ⚠️ **WARNING**
>
> Do not try to cut flush with the ground. It is too easy to have a kickback or dull your chain should you dig into the dirt. To remove the stump below ground level, see the box on the next page.

**9** **Follow procedure a second time**

**10** **Small, low stump remains**

# Cutting Down a Stump (continued)

## Completely Removing a Stump

When using a chainsaw, the closest you will probably be able to safely get to removing the stump is a couple of inches up from the ground level. But what if you do not want to see the stump at all? You have a number of options:

**Be patient (very patient).** Cover up the stump with some sod and keep it moist. Eventually it will rot, but it might take five to ten years. If it re-sprouts in the meantime, use an herbicide, such as Roundup, on the sprouts. You might hasten the rotting process by drilling one-inch diameter holes vertically into the stump. During the first year, fill the holes with a high-nitrogen fertilizer to encourage the growth of the organisms that decay the wood. After the first year, the organisms that decay the wood are carbon limited, so add granulated sugar into the holes.

**Chemicals.** Use a chemical made to encourage natural decomposition in stumps such as Stump-Out, Green Light's Stump Remover, or Revenge's Tree Stump Remover. To use these, drill one-inch diameter holes in the top and sides of the stump, add the granular chemicals and fill with water. The stump will start to become punky in four to twelve weeks and you can try to break it up with an ax. But do not expect miracles. Also, keep pets and kids away. These products contain some nasty chemicals such as potassium nitrate, sulfuric acid, and nitric acid. One other thing: These chemicals do not usually work on just-cut stumps. The stump should be dead for at least a year before these chemicals will actively start working.

**Burning.** Traditionally, stumps were burnt out. But before you go down that road, be sure it is legal in your community. (In many areas, it is not anymore.) And the problem is that once the wood ignites, it may burn for two to three weeks and you will need to monitor it closely. The result will likely be charcoal, which will not decompose, and you will end up having to dig it out anyway. Do not burn out a stump that is close to a building (such as the house in this project), woods, or grassy areas.

**Grubbing.** No, this does not refer to introducing insects (grubs) into the stump. It is the term used for digging around the stump and then trying to pull the whole stump out of the ground. It is a lot of work and I would not recommend it for stumps that are larger than about fourteen inches in diameter. The easiest way is to dig a trench around the stump, cut off the lateral roots, pry the stump to one side and then sever the taproot. Finally, you may need some kind of a winch to pull the stump out of the hole.

**Stump Grinding.** The method I recommend, it is the quickest and easiest— but unfortunately the most expensive. You can rent a stump grinder or have a tree service do it. The grinder is like a metal angle grinder with large teeth that chip the remaining stump into mulch. It can grind as deep as ten to twelve inches below grade and the grindings can be neatly raked back into the hole or removed. Within a matter of a few minutes, the stump will be an unseen memory. Depending on the size and location of the stump, a tree service may charge $100 to more than $1000 for this service.

PROJECT 11

# Milling Lumber from Logs

Attach guide board.

Board guides first cut.

Sawn surface guides cuts.

Beautiful lumber.

The process of turning logs into slabs or usable lumber, such as two by fours, is called milling. Although usually done commercially with a circular saw or band saw, milling can also be accomplished with a chainsaw and a special attachment.

There are two basic types of chainsaw mills—the frame type and the rail type. The name refers to the manner in which the chainsaw is guided to make its cut. (See more about rail mills in the box on page 161.) The best-known and most commonly used milling attachments are frame mills, often called Alaskan mills or slabbing mills.

These mills consist of a simple frame or guide that is connected to the chainsaw's guide bar. Setting the frame at differing distances from the bar allows various cutting depths to produce whatever thickness slab or lumber you desire. A variety of size mills are available starting under $150. One of the largest manufacturers of frame attachments and special ripping chain is Granberg International (*www.Granberg.com*).

Using a slabbing mill is not that difficult, but the process can be time-consuming and physically demanding. On large jobs, it is easier if you have two people working together.

⚠ **CAUTION**

Read and follow the instructions that come with your milling attachment.

Beautiful lumber can easily be cut with a milling attachment on a chainsaw.

# Milling Lumber from Logs Using a Frame Mill

## 1 Stabilize the log

**1 Stabilize the log.** First, I position the log at a comfortable working height and make sure it is secure and stable. This might be just on the ground with wedges placed under it to stabilize it. Then I find a flat guide board that is about eight inches wide and at least a foot longer than the log I will be milling. If the guide board is not straight and flat, your milled wood won't be flat either.

**2 Attach guide board.** I screw the guide board down to the top of the log with flathead screws, countersinking the screws flush or slightly below the surface of the board.

**3 Connect milling attachment.** Now, I attach the milling apparatus securely to my chainsaw and set the depth of the first cut. The model shown here clamps to the guide bar without drilling any holes.

## 2 Attach guide board

## 3 Connect milling attachment

# Milling Lumber from Logs Using a Frame Mill (continued)

**4 Cut first slab.** With the framework resting on top of the guide board and the chainsaw cutting below the board, I make an initial slabbing cut of about three inches thick. At first, this will feel awkward, but I quickly gained confidence with it.

> ### ⚠ CAUTION
>
> Be sure your initial slabbing cut is thick enough to miss the screws you drove in earlier.

**5 Maintain pressure during cut.**

For a flat cut, I move down the log, keeping pressure down on the framework with my right hand. Special ripping chain makes this job go a lot faster.

**4** Cut first slab

**5** Maintain pressure during cut

# Milling Lumber from Logs Using a Frame Mill *(continued)*

**6** Complete first cut

**6 Complete first cut.** I complete the first cut, hanging securely onto both the chainsaw and the framework. With a sharp chain, you should be able to plow through an eight-foot oak log in a couple of minutes.

**7 New flat surface revealed.** I lift off my guide board and the first slab to reveal a new and flat working surface.

**8 Set final slab thickness.** Setting the final slab thickness is quick and simple. My scrench fits the mill's bolts and the frame has a good inch scale on it.

**9 Flat surface eliminates guide board.** With a flat plane established on the log, I do not need the guide board. I can make successive cuts guiding the milling framework on the flat surface of the log. Make sure your guide bar is long enough to cut completely through the log.

**7** New flat surface revealed

# Milling Lumber from Logs Using a Frame Mill (continued)

**8** Set final slab thickness

**9** Flat surface eliminates guide board

# Milling Lumber from Logs Using a Frame Mill *(continued)*

**10** Maintaining slab thickness

**10 Maintaining slab thickness.** As long as I keep the thickness setting the same, each slab should be uniform in thickness. (Notice the first slab in the foreground.)

**11 Milling exposes grain and figure.** I have found some beautiful grain and character when milling my own lumber.

**11** Milling exposes grain and figure

## Rail Mills

Rail mills are an inexpensive alternative to frame mills. They consist of a small attachment fixed to the guide bar of the chainsaw. The attachment then rides on a rail attached to a log or slab.

Some attachments require pre-drilling of the bar, but others simply clamp on.

The attachment rides along a rail of wood or metal (shown here) that is screwed to your workpiece. Because the rails can be screwed on in any direction, you can cut the wood horizontally, vertically, or diagonally. Some rail mills have a feature that gives you the ability to make miter cuts and curved lines. They are a useful complement to the frame mill and can be purchased for under $100.

## The Original Lumbermaker

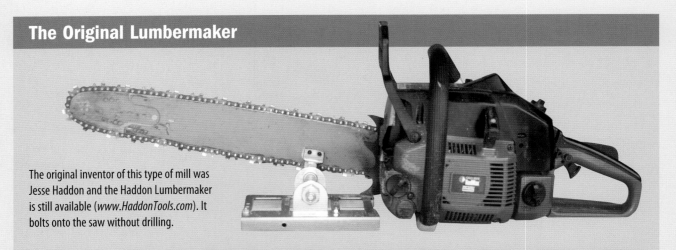

The original inventor of this type of mill was Jesse Haddon and the Haddon Lumbermaker is still available (*www.HaddonTools.com*). It bolts onto the saw without drilling.

To use the Lumbermaker, nail a 2 x 4 or 2 x 6 guide board to the top of the log and ride along the guide board.

Here I am using the Lumbermaker to edge a rough-cut slab previously sawn with a frame mill. The Board Master by Hudson (*www.Hud-son.com*) is similar to the Haddon Lumbermaker but requires drilling the guide bar on your chainsaw for the attachment. For an aluminum track and a lighter weight rail mill, look at the Mini Mill by Granberg International (*www.Granberg.com*).

## Bark Removal

One of the problems with using any mill is the damage cutting through bark can have on your chain. As if it were not bad enough that the wind packs dirt in all the cracks and crevices of the bark, the logs often have been rolled around in the mud, picking up even more cutter-dulling debris. If you are cutting dirty wood, it is common to need to sharpen your chain a number of times while milling a single large log.

It is best if you can remove the tree's bark before working on the log. This can be done with hand tools but it takes time and is hard work. Enter the chainsaw debarking attachment. The best-known brand is the Log Wizard. (For more information, go to *www. LogWizard.com*.)

The debarker is a three-inch wood planer set perpendicular to the bar and driven by the chain.

The debarker is a great attachment for preparing a log for milling as well as for grinding off knots and shaping convex surfaces.

## PROJECT 12

# When to Bring in a Professional

Heavy limb ready to fall.

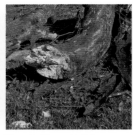
The wind brought it down.

Safe to saw now.

Bucked into firewood.

It is not unusual to start a chainsaw project and then discover it is beyond your capabilities. Just because you know how to start and operate a chainsaw does not mean you can safely perform every task. In some cities, you have to be trained, licensed, and specially insured to do tree work. Know your limits. I believe you should call in an experienced professional whenever:

■ a situation requires more skills than you have.

■ a tree has a larger diameter than the length of the guide bar on your chainsaw.

■ the tree is dead, hollow, split, or rotten.

■ the tree you want to work on is partially uprooted and not completely down.

■ the tree you are felling gets hung up in another tree.

■ you would have to work from a ladder or climb in the tree.

■ there is not enough room to safely fell the tree or there is no clear escape route.

Following is an example of when to call in a professional.

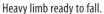

There are many difficult situations when it's best to cover your chainsaw's bar and call in a licensed tree professional. This tree contains a large broken limb that has not let go. It is too high for me to reach and too heavy to risk working below.

# When to Bring in a Professional

**1** Know when to bring in a professional

### 1 Know when to bring in a professional.

Looking up into this large storm-damaged tree, it is obvious there is a lot of dead wood. This big limb is broken, but has not entirely let go of the trunk. Somebody tried to hold the tree together with steel cable—if the cable does not catch in the saw's chain, it is liable to wrap around it. Too risky for me. I found a professional who offered to come out with his truck lift and take it down for $150. That is a bargain.

### 2 Wind brings it down.

That night the wind came up and Mother Nature saved me $150. It is a good thing there was nobody below it. The falling limb probably would have killed them. By good luck, a nearby garage also was spared.

### 3 When it's on the ground, cut it.

Once the branch was safely on the ground, I could do the work myself bucking it up into firewood lengths.

**2** Wind brings it down

# When to Bring in a Professional (continued)

# CHAPTER 6

# Maintenance, Service, and Sharpening

Regular cleaning, maintenance, and sharpening of your chainsaw will ensure a relatively trouble-free life. Many procedures should be performed at the end of every day's use. Others should be performed every couple of weeks, with additional maintenance required when putting your chainsaw away for the season. Of course, the amount and timing of maintenance will be different if you are a heavy user or a weekend warrior. But no matter how often you use your saw, do not neglect its maintenance and just throw it in the back of your truck or on a shelf in your garage at the end of the day. Every day that I use one of my chainsaws, I reserve some maintenance and sharpening time before I finish for the day.

A sharp chain is particularly important, and you may need to field sharpen during a day of cutting. You'll know because the saw will make dust, not chips. A dull chain is not only slower and harder to use, it's also dangerous because you will be putting undue stress on the saw mechanism, and you are liable to bind the chain in the saw cut.

Removing the oil cap and checking the filter is part of a regular maintenance schedule.

## Maintenance Tools

Gathering up the necessary tools and keeping them together is one way of encouraging the maintenance and service to be done. I bought a separate set of tools and a tool box and use them just for chainsaw maintenance so I don't have to dig around my workshop for tools. Maintenance is a small investment that will pay off with a better-running saw.

Here is my basic list of tools. Your specific saw may require other specialty tools. (See page 189 for tools for sharpening.)

- Owner's manual
- Tight-fitting leather gloves
- Safety glasses or goggles
- Stiff bristle brush
- Small brass brush
- Spark plug gap gauge
- Small piece of hooked wire or "hooking tool"
- Small engineer's square
- Flat file for metal
- Metal scraper or putty knife
- Wrenches to fit your chainsaw
- Screwdrivers to fit your chainsaw
- White lithium grease
- Cleaning rags
- Toolbox to hold tools

## Maintenance Schedule

In the charts at right you will find my recommendations for a maintenance schedule with references to how-to photos on the following pages. How heavily you use your saw will determine your maintenance schedule, but do not neglect it.

There is always one other thing to check out. Consult your owner's manual for your manufacturer's maintenance and service recommendations in case they are different from the guidelines I am suggesting here.

Sharpening the chain on your saw, of course, is one of the most important steps of maintenance. For that reason, it is covered separately starting on page 186.

### Electric- vs. Gas-Powered Chainsaws

There is considerably less maintenance required on an electric-powered saw than a gas-powered saw (no spark plug, starter reel, and air, fuel, and oil filters). But that does not mean that an electric-powered saw is maintenance-free. You should be as diligent about going through the same steps of tensioning and examining the guide bar and sharpening the chain, as well as wiping the saw clean on a regular basis. In addition, carefully examine the power cord, extension cord, plugs, and "ON/OFF" switch for any damage. An electric short can be fatal.

## Maintenance/Service

## How-To Guide? (Figure numbers refer to photos on the following pages)

### After Every Use

| Maintenance/Service | How-To Guide |
|---|---|
| **Clean thoroughly** | Wipe and brush dirt and debris from saw body (pay particular attention to the engine cylinder cooling fins). |
| **Check for loose screws, nuts** | Tighten if needed (pay particular attention to the chain catcher and chain brake handle). |
| **Inspect chain** | Look for damaged or worn cutters, links or rivets. Replace chain if necessary. |
| **Inspect sharpness of chain** | Sharpen if needed. See pages 186–191. |
| **Inspect chain brake** | Remove guide bar and chain. Clean brake band. See **Figures 1–3**. |
| **Clean oil hole** | See **Figure 4**. |
| **Clean clutch drum** | See **Figure 5**. |
| **Inspect outside edges of guide bar rails for burrs** | File off burrs. See **Figure 6**. |
| **Inspect guide bar edges for bluing or a pinched bar slot** | Replace bar. See **Figure 7**. |
| **Clean out bar slot** | See **Figure 8**. |
| **Clean out holes in mounting end of bar** | See **Figure 9**. |
| **If nose has sprocket tip, check for ease of rotation** | If sprocket doesn't spin easily, clean out any debris. Grease. See **Figure 11**. |
| **Reassemble the guide bar and chain** | When reassembling bar, flip it 180 degrees to ensure uniform wear on opposite rails. |
| **Check chain tension** | To re-tension guide bar and chain, see pages 54-57 in Chapter 4. |
| **Inspect and clean air filter** | See **Figures 12–17**. |
| **Clean around carburetor, adjusting screws, and choke** | Avoid getting dirt in the carburetor throat. |
| **Replace the air filter and the cover plate** | See **Figure 18**. |

### After 50 Hours of Use

| Maintenance/Service | How-To Guide |
|---|---|
| **Check condition of anti-vibration mounts** | Check for looseness or deterioration. |
| **Remove cover plate and inspect spark arrestor** | Look for tears or holes and remove exhaust build up. See **Figures 19–21**. |
| **Check chain brake** | Remove chain brake from head. See **Figure 23**. |
| **Check clutch and sprocket** | Clean debris from clutch and sprocket and inspect sprocket for wear. See **Figures 23** and **24**. |
| **Inspect guide bar** | Look for twisting or bends. Check for square. See **Figure 25**. Check for spread rails. See **Figure 26**. |
| **Check bar groove depth** | Use ruler. See **Figure 27**. |
| **Check mounting end of guide bar** | Check lead-ins. See **Figure 28**. |
| **Inspect/clean/replace spark plug** | See **Figures 29–36**. |
| **Inspect recoil starter and rope** | See **Figures 37–40**. |
| **Clean vanes and fins** | See **Figure 41**. |
| **Inspect fuel system** | Empty fuel tank and inspect filter. See **Figures 42** and **43**. Wash out tank with fuel/oil mix if needed. |
| **Inspect oil system** | See **Figures 44–47**. |
| **Tune the engine** | See sidebar on page 185. |

### For the Season

| Maintenance/Service | How-To Guide |
|---|---|
| **Empty the gas tank** | Use up fuel by sawing, or empty into an appropriate container. Start the saw repeatedly to use up fuel in the lines. |
| **Add oil to cylinder** | Remove spark plug, and add a teaspoon of 2-cycle oil or cylinder rust inhibitor into the cylinder. Pull starter rope slowly several times to distribute the oil, then replace spark plug. |
| **Store saw in a dry location to prevent rust** | Remove chain and store in a container of oil. Give bar a light coat of oil and wrap in paper. |

# Maintenance How-To Guide

## CHAIN BRAKE

CHAPTER 6: MAINTENANCE, SERVICE, AND SHARPENING

**1** Clean cover plate's interior

Cover plate

**1** Remove the cover plate. Clean dirt and gunk off the inside where the bar mounts. I'm using a putty knife as a scraper.

**2** Clean housing exterior

Brake housing system

**2** Clean the outside of the brake housing with a stiff brush. Clean the inside of the cover plate where the chain brake is located.

**3** Clean brake housing

Brake housing

**3** Use a rag to clean dust and oil from the inside of the brake housing. Pay particular attention to the round metal brake band.

 **⚠ CAUTION**

Check the chain brake by revving the saw, then pushing the hand guard forward. The saw should stop instantly. If the chain brake does not operate correctly, have it adjusted or repaired by an authorized service technician before operating your saw again.

**4** Clean around oil hole

**4** Use the putty knife to clean dirt away from the guide bar mounting area. Brush dirt out of the oil slot.

# Maintenance How-To Guide *(continued)*

## GUIDE BAR

### 5 Clean clutch drum

File

Guide bar

Clutch drum

**5** Thoroughly clean the outside of the clutch drum with a bristle brush, then remove any oil residue with a clean rag.

### 6 Remove guide bar burrs

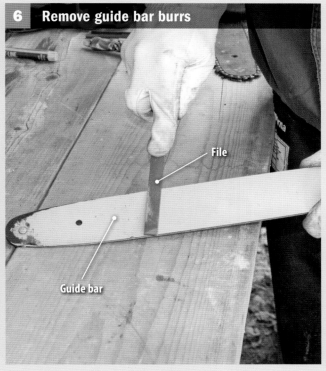

File

Guide bar

**6** Remove burrs from the guide bar by filing toward the body with a flat file.

### 7 When to replace the guide bar

**7** Note the obvious normal wear, such as the divot in front of my finger. A blued area along the guide rail indicates a pinched bar slot. If you notice these things, it's time to replace the bar.

### 8 Cleaning bar slot

**8** Use a bar-groove cleaning tool or your putty knife to clean dirt out of the bar slot. Work from the sprocket tip toward the chain entry slot.

# Maintenance How-To Guide *(continued)*

## 9 Clean oil and mounting holes

**9** Use the bar-groove cleaning tool or some other metal pick to clean out the oil holes and adjusting screw pin hole in the mounting end of the guide bar.

## 10 Reassemble saw and tension chain

**10** Before reassembling the saw, turn the guide bar adjusting screw counter-clockwise two turns to ease refitting the guide bar. You can flip the guide bar over to ensure uniform wear.

## 11 Lubricate sprocket tip

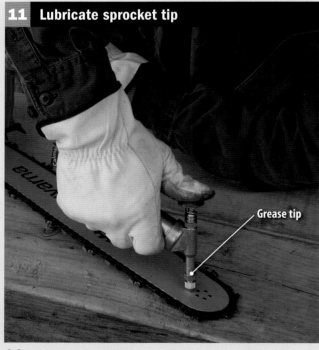

Grease tip

**11** Use a grease gun to lubricate sprocket tip with regular lithium grease.

## To Grease or Not to Grease?

Bar and chain oil is usually adequate to lubricate the sprocket tip, but some users like to grease as well. To grease or not to grease? That is the question. Here is the debate as I understand it. Greasing your sprocket nose will lubricate better than oil and a packing of grease around the bearings will help keep dirt out of them, prolonging their life. If greased religiously or consistently, this is the best scenario. However, though a full packing of grease will keep dirt out, a very light packing will trap dirt in around the bearings. Bar oil will be unable to flush this dirt and it will cause more harm than not greasing. If you grease, grease often and keep with it, or do not grease at all.

# Maintenance How-To Guide (continued)

## AIR FILTER

**12  Removing air filter cover plate**

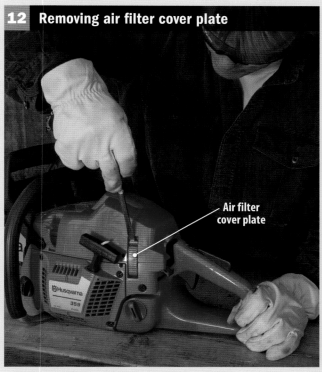

Air filter
cover plate

**12**  Remove the air filter cover plate.

**13  Attachment method varies**

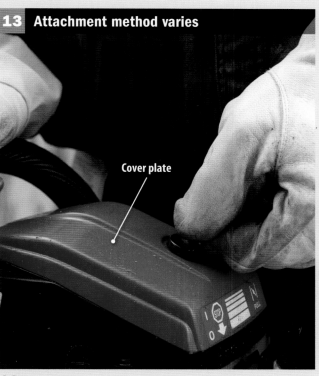

Cover plate

**13**  Your saw may have screws, clips, a lever, or large thumbscrew holding the cover plate.

**14  Access air filter**

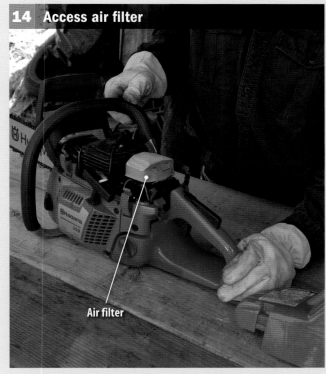

Air filter

**14**  With the cover plate removed, you can easily access the air filter.

**15  Keep debris out of carburetor**

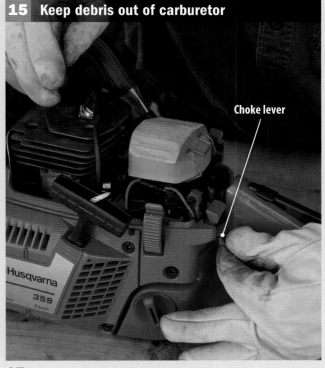

Choke lever

**15**  Before removing the air filter, pull the choke lever to prevent debris from entering the carburetor.

# Maintenance How-To Guide *(continued)*

## 16 Remove air filter

**16** Remove the air filter.

## 17 Clean air filter

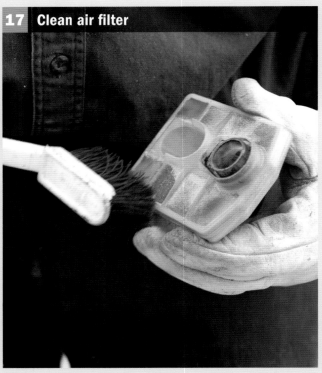

**17** Use a brush and/or compressed air to clean out the filter, blowing from the clean side of the filter. Refer to your owner's manual for the replacement filter order number or to determine if your filter requires a different cleaning procedure.

## SPARK ARRESTOR

## 18 Replace air filter

Air filter

**18** Replace the air filter. Never start an engine without an air filter or with one that is damaged.

## 19 Check spark arrestor screen

Spark arrestor

Retaining screw

**19** With the cover plate removed and adequate lighting, look into the exhaust port(s) of the muffler for a buildup of carbon on the spark arrestor screen.

# Maintenance How-To Guide (continued)

## 20 Remove spark arrestor screen

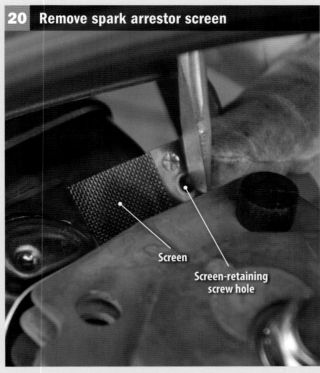

Screen

Screen-retaining screw hole

**20** If you see a buildup of carbon blocking the mesh, remove the screen-retaining screw and the screen.

## 21 Clean spark arrestor screen

A brass brush may be necessary

**21** If screen is clogged, clean it with a brass brush. A propane torch may also be used to burn off exhaust buildup, but do not do this near any flammable fuel or the saw itself.

## DRIVE SPROCKETS

## 22 Inspect sliding surfaces

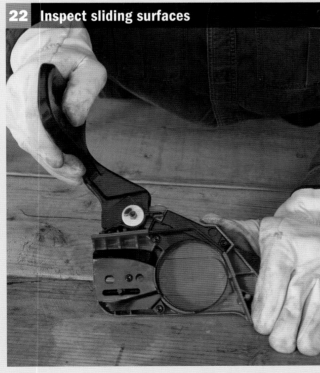

**22** Inspect sliding surfaces and pivot points of chain brake for adequate lubrication. If necessary, use white lithium grease or check owner's manual for proper lubricant.

## 23 Chain wear on rim-type sprockets

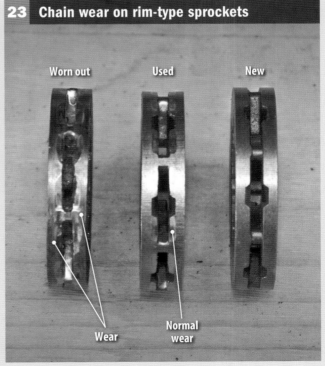

Worn out    Used    New

Wear

Normal wear

**23** Note the major grooves in the sprocket on the left caused by the chain. Replace chain and have a new sprocket installed by an authorized service technician.

# Maintenance How-To Guide (continued)

### 24 Chain wear on spur-type sprockets

New sprocket

Worn sprocket

Worn out sprocket

**24** The sprocket on the left is new. The center sprocket is worn. The sprocket on the right needs to be replaced. These are spur (gear) type sprockets, which, unlike rim sprockets, are welded to the clutch drum. Most homeowner saws have this type of sprocket.

## GUIDE BAR

### 25 Ensure guide bar is straight

Guide bar

Square

### 26 Check for rail spread

**25** Sight down both sides of the bar to check that it is straight. Use a small square against the face of the bar to make sure the rails run at right angles to the bar body. Sometimes you can repair a bar by filing the rail sides, but if the bar is bent or beat, replace it.

**26** Hold a straight edge from the center of the bar to the side of a cutting tooth. Try to force the cutter sideways with the straight edge. If the cutter moves over far enough for the straight edge to lie flat against the bar, then the bar needs to be replaced. This bar's rails are not spread or worn, as indicated by the wedge of light between the straight edge and the bar face.

# Maintenance How-To Guide (continued)

### 27 Measure groove depth

**27** Measure bar groove depth to ensure the clearance between the drive link of the chain and bottom of the bar groove is maintained at 1mm. Here the bar groove depth is ⁷/₃₂ inch or 5.5mm so the drive link on the chain must be no more than ¹¹/₆₄ inch or 4.5mm.

### 28 Inspect lead-ins

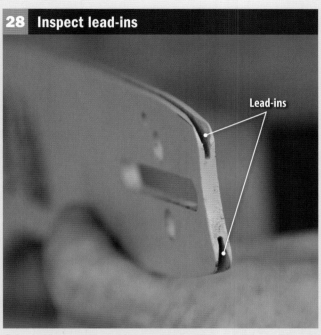

Lead-ins

**28** Inspect the lead-ins at the mounting end of the guide bar. They should be slightly funnel-shaped to allow smooth acceptance of the drive links. File if needed.

## SPARK PLUG

### 29 Remove spark plug cover

Spark plug

Plug wire

**29** To inspect the spark plug, first remove the top cover plate and then pull off the plug wire.

 **CAUTION**

Before removing the spark plug, clean any debris from around it. Never allow anything to fall into the spark plug hole.

### 30 Loosen spark plug

**30** Turn the spark plug counterclockwise with the combination wrench that came with your saw or a proper-sized socket wrench.

# Maintenance How-To Guide *(continued)*

### 31 Remove spark plug

**31** After the spark plug has been loosened with a wrench, remove it the rest of the way by hand.

### 32 Clean spark plug

**32** Clean any deposits with a brass brush. Then, inspect the electrodes for deterioration and replace a damaged or worn spark plug.

## Spark Plugs Tell A Story

Rich fuel mix     Lean fuel mix     Correct fuel mix     New plug

Once a spark plug has been removed, take a good look at it, because it can give you some hints as to how your engine is operating.

The plug on the left is dark brown or almost black, indicating the engine is getting too much fuel and not enough air (a rich mixture). A blocked air filter, an incorrect carburetor adjustment, or an incorrect fuel mixture could cause it.

The white or light deposits on the second plug from the left indicate a lean mixture (too much air, not enough fuel). This could be caused by an air leak between the carburetor and cylinder, possibly from a failed gasket or loose carburetor screw, an incorrect carburetor adjustment, an incorrect fuel mixture, or a clogged fuel filter.

A grey or light brown plug such as the third from the left indicates a properly adjusted carburetor and fuel mixture. For comparison, the plug on the right is a brand new spark plug.

While you have the spark plug removed, inspect the ceramic casing for cracks, discoloration, or distortion. Replace it if you have any concerns. A bad spark plug is one of the top causes of engine malfunction, and replacing one will not cost you an arm and a leg.

# Maintenance How-To Guide (continued)

### 33 Check electrode gap

Gapping tool

**33** Check the electrode gap with an automotive gapping tool to make sure that it meets the manufacturer's recommendation.

### 34 Oil plug threads

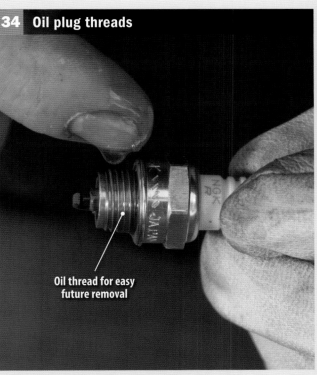

Oil thread for easy future removal

**34** Before reinstalling the plug, clean the threads and put a small drop of bar oil on them to aid in future removal.

### 35 Re-install spark plug

**35** When installing a spark plug, always start threading it in with your fingers until the gasket reaches the cylinder head. Then, using the wrench, tighten it about an eighth to a quarter turn more. Do not overtighten.

### 36 Replace spark plug wire

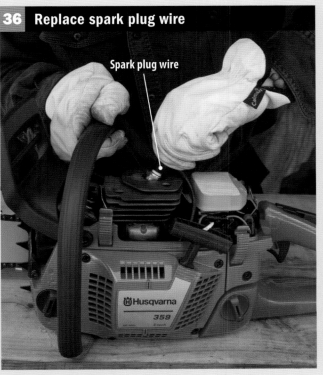

Spark plug wire

**36** Finally, replace the plug wire securely and secure the top cover.

# Maintenance How-To Guide *(continued)*

**37** **Check starter rope for fraying**

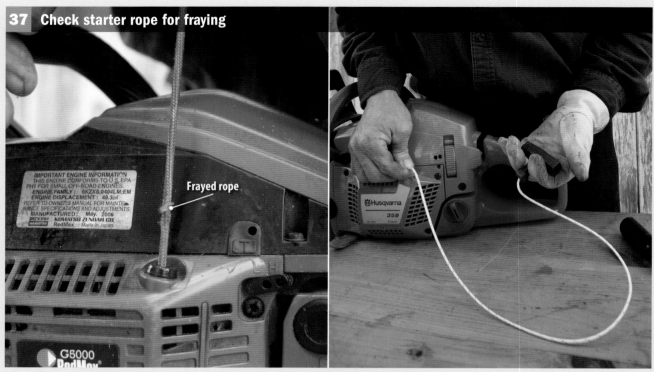

Frayed rope

**37** Pull the starter handle to fully extend the rope and check it for fraying. If you find anything worse than very light fraying from normal wear, replace the rope.

## RECOIL STARTER

**38** **Remove recoil starter housing**

Recoil starter housing

**38** Remove the recoil starter housing by removing the retaining screws or by following the instructions in your owner's manual.

**39** **Clean recoil mechanism**

Recoil starting mechanism

**39** Use a stiff brush to clean dust and debris from the recoil starting mechanism.

# Maintenance How-To Guide (continued)

## 40 Check starter rope tension

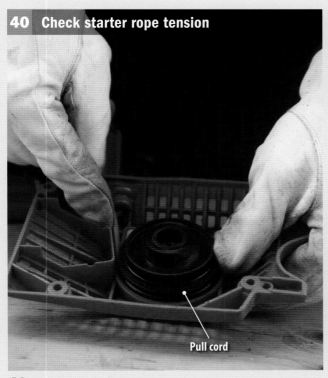

Pull cord

**40** The starter handle should fit snugly against the housing. If it doesn't, pull some rope from the reel as I am doing in the photo. Then wrap that section of rope around the reel to increase rope tension. Be careful—there's a spring in here that's liable to go "sproing."

## 41 Clean engine cooling fins

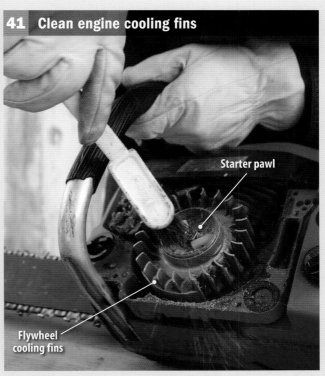

Starter pawl

Flywheel cooling fins

**41** Brush dust and debris from the engine cooling fins and surrounding casing with a scraper and wire brush. Dirty fins can lead to overheating.

## FUEL FILTER

## 42 Remove fuel filter

Fuel filter

**42** When the fuel tank runs empty, remove the cap and use a hooked wire or hook tool to fish the fuel filter from the gas tank.

## 43 Inspect fuel filter

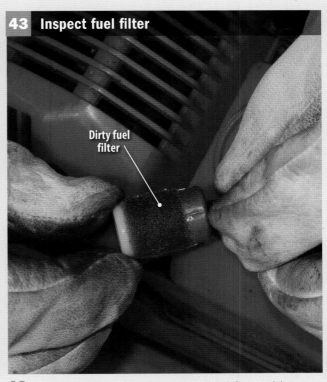

Dirty fuel filter

**43** Inspect the fuel filter. If it is dirty or clogged with fine wood dust, replace it.

# Maintenance How-To Guide *(continued)*

## OIL FILTER

**44 Remove oil cap**

**44** Remove the oil cap from the oil tank.

**45 Remove oil filter**

**45** Use a hooked wire or tool to fish the oil filter from the tank.

**46 Inspect oil filter**

**46** Inspect the oil filter for accumulated gunk. If it is dirty, clean or replace it.

**47 Adjust oil pump**

**47** Adjust oil pump. Some saws have an adjustable oil pump. It may need to be adjusted to suit the length of a new guide bar, the size of the wood you are cutting, or the hardness of the wood. On most saws, the adjustment screw is accessed from the underside. Usually, there is a small symbol indicating which way to turn the screw for more or less oil.

# Maintenance How-To Guide (continued)

## Engine Tuning ... and When It's Time to Call in the Pros

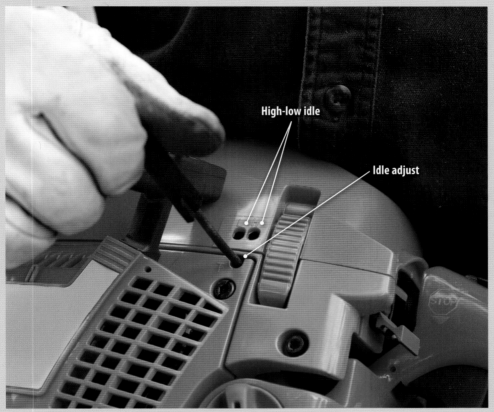

High-low idle

Idle adjust

To set the idle, turn the screw slowly counterclockwise until the chain stops moving.

After inspecting and cleaning your chainsaw, reassemble all of the parts to check the carburetor adjustment settings. For the engine to be tuned, all of the parts (air and fuel flow, fuel mix, spark plug, and ignition system) must be working properly. To check that it is properly tuned, start your chainsaw and allow it to run for a minute or two to warm it up. Rev the engine periodically while it is warming up.

While it is idling (and the chain brake is off), the chain should not move around the bar. If it does, the idle screw should be slowly turned counterclockwise (see photo above) until the chain stops moving. If you can't make this happen, take your saw into a qualified technician for service.

With the saw still idling and the chain brake still off, pull the throttle trigger quickly and hold in for a second. The engine should respond quickly. If it bogs down before increasing in speed, a service technician should adjust the carburetor.

Finally, with the chain brake off, hold the throttle trigger in fully until the saw achieves maximum speed. If this sounds faster or slower than when you initially bought your saw, the carburetor's high-speed jet may need to be adjusted by a service technician using a tachometer.

Incorrect adjustment of the carburetor high-low idle screws can lead to engine failure.

# Sharpening the chain

When the saw chain makes hot dust instead of wood chips, it's dull and needs to be sharpened. Even if you keep your chain out of the dirt and cut clean wood, your chain will eventually lose its sharp edge. Professional loggers will sharpen their saws multiple times throughout the day. This may be a mere one or two file strokes per cutter, but once you get used to a sharp chain and a fast cutting saw, the time you'll spend on a quick field sharpening makes up for the time wasted by a slow-cutting saw.

A dull chain is not only taxing to the bar, sprocket, engine, and operator, but poses a safety risk as well, because it is liable to bind on the log and may break. A few minutes learning to sharpen your chain will be well worth the investment when it comes to cutting. You can sharpen with a powered system or manually.

## POWERED SHARPENING

There are several motorized sharpening systems available. They can be 12 volt to run off your vehicle, battery powered, or use 110-volt household current. See top photo at right.

They can be as simple as a handheld motor with a small cylindrical sharpening stone or as complex as a bench mount system. See bottom photo. All of the motorized sharpening systems come with complete instructions that you should be sure to follow.

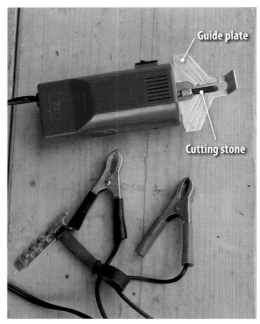

Guide plate

Cutting stone

This 12-volt handheld sharpener will run off your vehicle's battery. Be sure it has a guide plate and change the cutting stone when it starts thinning.

If you do a lot of cutting, consider a bench grinder like this one from Oregon (*www.OregonChain.com*). Look for one that is fully adjustable for different chain sizes.

## MANUAL SHARPENING

Manual sharpening is the cheapest, quickest, and, I believe, the best way to sharpen your chain. It can be done in the field with the chain on the saw, and removes the least amount of cutter material, so it lengthens the life of your chain. And, with the help of a few gauges and tools, sharpening really is not that difficult.

When you sharpen manually, after every five or so sharpenings you may need to have your chain professionally sharpened, or use your own power sharpener, to return it to a truly uniform machined edge. But the time and chain life you will save by hand filing will be well worth the effort and convenience. I've got a little saying: "It's always better to file a little bit and often, than to file a lot, occasionally."

Here are the items needed to manually sharpen your chain:

- Round file with a handle (check owner's manual for correct size)
- Matching file guide/holder
- Flat file with a handle (check owner's manual for correct size)
- Matching depth gauge
- Calipers
- Bench vise or stump vise
- Crayon, chalk, or felt tip marker
- Bristle brush
- Tight-fitting leather gloves
- Safety glasses

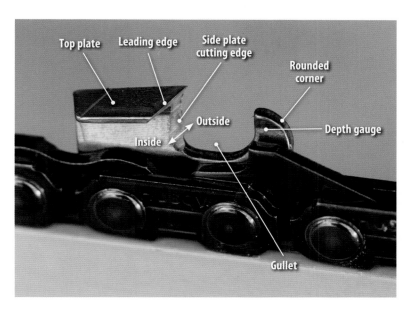

### ⚠ CAUTION

**Before you sharpen a chain, check that:**

- Stop switch is in the off position. (If it is an electric-powered saw, it should be unplugged.)
- Spark plug wire is disconnected.
- Chain is tensioned properly and clean of oil, grease, and wood chips.
- There are no cracked or broken tie straps and cutters, or worn or loose rivets. (If you can rotate rivets with your fingers, they are too loose.)
- You are wearing tight-fitting leather gloves.

# Manual Sharpening: Step-by-Step

**1 Secure the saw**

Stump vise

**2 Clean dust and debris from chain**

**3 Pick starting point**

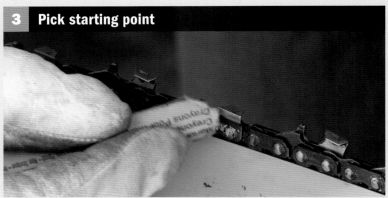

**4 Secure the file handle**

**5 Put file in filing gauge**

**1 Secure the saw.** Secure the saw bar in a vise so you have access to the chain and it can still move. Here, the vise is a portable stump vise that is hammered into the end grain of a stump.

**2 Clean dust and debris from chain.** Clean any dust or debris out of the chain with a small bristle brush. Rotate the chain as you clean.

**3 Pick starting point.** Find the smallest or most damaged cutter as your starting point. Mark the starting point. Clearly mark that cutter with a crayon, chalk, or felt-tip marker so you know where you started.

**4 Secure the file handle.** Mount and secure the handle on the round file. For a wooden handle, force the handle over the tang of the file and tap with a mallet.

**5 Put file in filing gauge.** Slide or clip the round file into the filing gauge.

# Manual Sharpening: Step-by-Step (continued)

**6 Determine filing angle.** Check with your owner's manual or the chain manufacturer for the top plate filing angle (usually twenty-five, thirty, or thirty-five degrees) and align the mark (here thirty degrees) so that it is parallel with the guide bar and chain.

**7 Holding the file guide.** Hold the file guide at a ninety-degree angle to the flat face of the saw bar. Some manufacturers specify holding the guide ten degrees down from square at the file handle. This type of file guide is designed to ride on the cutter and the depth gauge.

**8 File from inside to outside.** File from the inside of the cutters to the outside while maintaining the correct angle throughout the stroke. Apply pressure on the forward stroke only. Continue filing (usually two to five strokes) until the top cutting edge is clean and sharp and the smooth chromed edge of the cutter extends to the top and the side plate cutting edges.

**9 Sharpen, measure each cutter.** This cutter tooth is now your marker, and you can use a caliper to check that the others are filed the same. After each cutter has been sharpened, move the chain forward and sharpen the next cutter on that side. When you reach your marked cutter, move to the other side of the chain to sharpen that side's cutters as well. Keep all cutters uniform.

**6 Determine filing angle**

**7 Holding the file guide**

**8 File from inside to outside**

**9 Sharpen, measure each cutter**

## Filing the cutters and depth gauges

### Sharpening the cutting edges

Turn the chain-tension screw clockwise until the chain is tight and rigid. Lay the file guide horizontally across the top of the chain so that the file fits against a cutter's curved, beveled cutting edge, and the top plate and the depth gauge support the guide. Align the appropriate angle-marker line with the edge of the guide bar and push steadily forward, applying moderate pressure against the cutting edge. Repeat the same forward stroke two or three times. Do not apply pressure to the cutting edge on the return stroke.

File all of the cutters that have similarly angled cutting edges—every other cutter on the chain. Then, switch the angle of the file guide and go on to file the remaining cutters.

### Filing the depth gauges

Check the depth gauge on each cutter after you have sharpened its cutting edge. Set the depth gauge tool over the top of the chain as shown, the back edge of its grooved toe butting against the inside edge of the depth gauge. If the depth gauge protrudes, hold a single-cut mill file horizontal and perpendicular to the chain and push the file lightly across the top of the depth gauge. Lift the file and return it to the starting position. Do not pull the file back across the metal edge. Continue filing until the top edge of the depth gauge is level with the surface of the depth gauge tool. Remove the tool and round off the outer corner of the depth gauge with a few light strokes, again filing only on the forward stroke.

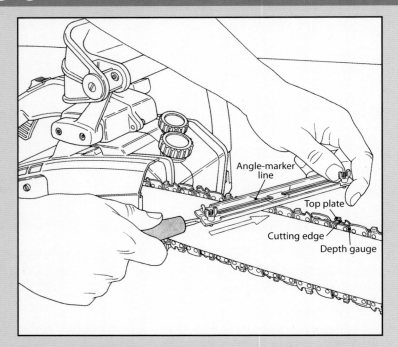

Angle-marker line

Top plate

Cutting edge

Depth gauge

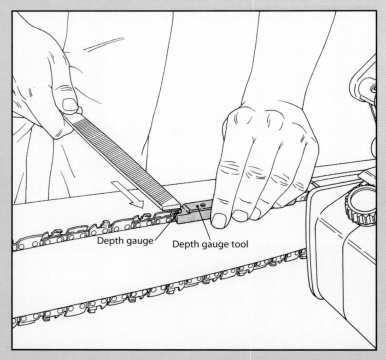

Depth gauge    Depth gauge tool

CHAPTER 6: MAINTENANCE, SERVICE, AND SHARPENING

# Manual Sharpening: Step-by-Step (continued)

**10 Check chain's depth gauge.** As cutters are filed back, their height is diminished in relation to the depth gauges. The depth gauges must be checked every three or four sharpenings. If they are too high, the chain will not bite easily. Follow the manufacturer's recommendation for correct depth gauge setting. Never over-file depth gauges, as this can lead to kickback!

**11 Using the gauge tool.** Place the depth gauge tool over at least two cutters. Make sure the depth gauge on the chain enters the slot of the depth gauge tool. If the depth gauge protrudes, it is too high and needs to be filed down.

**12 Filing the depth gauge.** Using a flat file and level strokes, file the depth gauge down to the level of the depth gauge tool. Use flat forward strokes from the inside out.

**13 Round the depth gauge.** Use the depth gauge tool to protect the sharpened cutter while you round off the front corner of the depth gauge with the flat file. Continue to file and round all depth gauges.

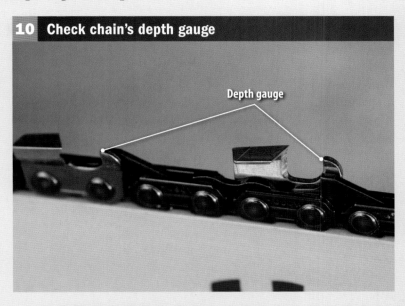

**10  Check chain's depth gauge**

Depth gauge

**11  Using the gauge tool**

**12  Filing the depth gauge**

**13  Round the depth gauge**

## APPENDIX A:
# How a Chainsaw Works

Though a toothed chain does the cutting, the heart of any chainsaw is the gas-powered engine or electric motor, so we will start there. It gives the chain the power to travel at speeds up to 4,000 to 6,000 feet per minute.

### ENGINES AND MOTORS

Gas-powered saws are started with the pull of a starter cord that turns the crankshaft. This, in turn, moves the piston in and out of the combustion chamber (unlike an automobile, chainsaws have a single piston and a two-stroke cycle.)

In the combustion chamber, as the piston rises, it compresses the fuel, the spark plug fires, and the fuel ignites. The combustion pushes the piston downward, allowing the exhaust gases to escape and forcing some of the fuel-air mixture from the crankcase into the combustion chamber. And then a new cycle begins. At full throttle, a chainsaw engine can run from 6,000 to 14,500 revolutions per minute (RPM).

Electric-powered chainsaws simply have a standard electric or battery-operated motor that powers the chain. They are generally sized from 1hp to 3hp.

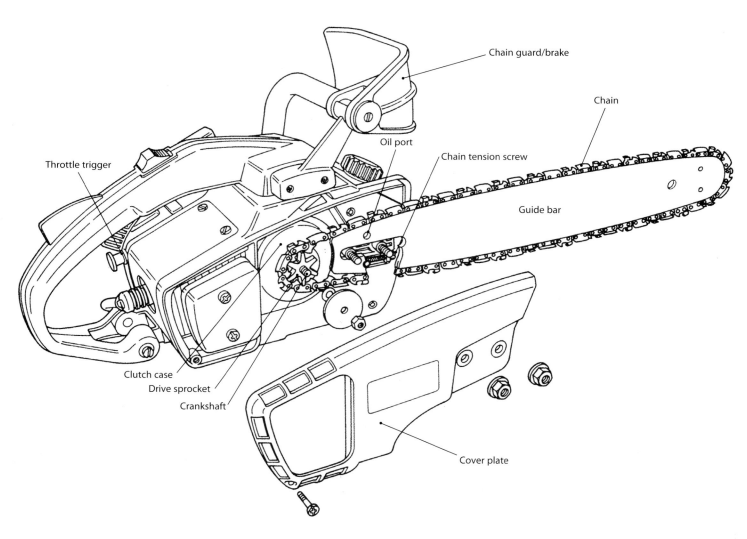

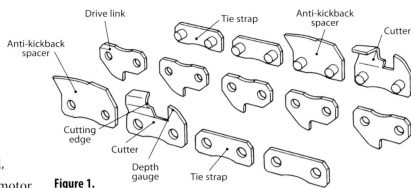

**Figure 1.**

Labels on Figure 1: Drive link, Tie strap, Anti-kickback spacer, Cutter, Anti-kickback spacer, Cutting edge, Cutter, Depth gauge, Tie strap

## CLUTCH AND DRIVE SPROCKET

When the throttle trigger is depressed, power from the chainsaw's engine or motor spins the drive shaft. Mounted on the drive shaft is a clutch. The clutch plays an important safety role since it permits the chain to spin only when the operator pulls the trigger throttle enough to start cutting.

The entire assembly works on the principle of centrifugal force, so that only when the engine speed reaches a specified number of RPMs (usually 2,500 – 3,500) do the clutch shoes spinning on the drive shaft push outward enough to engage and turn the clutch case or drum.

Attached to the clutch case is a gear called the drive sprocket. As the clutch case spins at full throttle, so does the drive sprocket, and, consequently, the chain that is wrapped around the sprocket.

The reverse happens when the operator releases the throttle. The drive shaft slows, the centrifugal force decreases, and the clutch shoes are drawn together by a circular spring. The shoes disengage from the clutch case, and the drive sprocket and chain stop spinning.

## CHAIN

Small teeth on a linked chain, like a bicycle chain, carry out the cutting action. The chain travels around a steel guide bar.

The chain is constructed of three strands of hardened-steel links. See **Figure 1**. They are riveted together to form one continuous loop. The middle strand consists of a series of drive links whose hook-shaped bottom edges fit into the slot along the edge of the guide bar. The thickness of the drive link is called

the chain gauge. Most homeowner saws have a .050 inch gauge chain. The hooks on the bottom of the drive links also engage the teeth on the drive sprocket, so it is their job to move the chain along its course.

On both sides of the middle strand are strands of steel that include the actual cutters, spacers, and tie straps that hold the chain together.

Every other cutter is sharpened the opposite direction. See **Figure 2**. The distance from the outside of a left-hand cutter to the outside of a right-hand cutter will determine the width of the cut (the kerf). The other important chain measurement is its pitch.

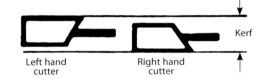

Labels on Figure 2: Kerf, Left hand cutter, Right hand cutter

**Figure 2.** Saw chain kerf.

It's usually measured with a caliper spanning three rivets; then, divide this measurement by two. Most homeowner saws come with ⅜ pitch (.375 pitch) chain.

**Figure 3.** Measure pitch by spanning three rivets with a caliper, then divide by two. This is because tie straps and cutters aren't always equal in size.

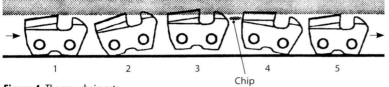

**Figure 4.** The saw chain cuts wood when the cutter tooth actually leaves the guide bar to bite into the wood and remove a wood chip.

It is usually assumed that the cutter teeth ride tight along the guide bar at all times, but that is not actually true. See **Figure 4**.

All saw chain cuts have a rocking motion. When cutting properly, a saw chain resembles a dolphin swimming in the ocean. As the cutter enters the wood, the leading (or cutting) edge starts to bite (1) causing the cutter to rock back as far as the depth gauge will allow (2). The cutter is now in the attack position and jumps off the guide bar and into the wood (3). Next, chain tension and power from the saw pull the cutter back out of the wood and the severed chip exits from the underside of the cutter (4). The cutter then returns to its original position (5).

There are two important parts on each cutter tooth. See **Figure 5**. First is the cutting (leading) edge. But just as important is the depth gauge. The depth gauge is the rounded forward edge that sits in front of the cutting edge and determines how far the cutter will rock back in position and ultimately how large a bite the cutter will take.

The top of the depth gauge must be lower than the leading (cutting) edge. If it is not, the cutter will not be able to take a bite. But if the depth gauge is too low in relation to the leading edge, the rocking motion will become very rough and will force the cutter to take an over-sized bite. The cutter can grab the wood and the engine might stall or the chain might break. It can also lead to severe pull-in, pull-back, and kickback. It is important that as you sharpen the leading edge and the top plate you also lower the depth gauge in the same proportion. (For more about sharpening, see pages 186–191).

**Figure 5.** The cutter tooth.

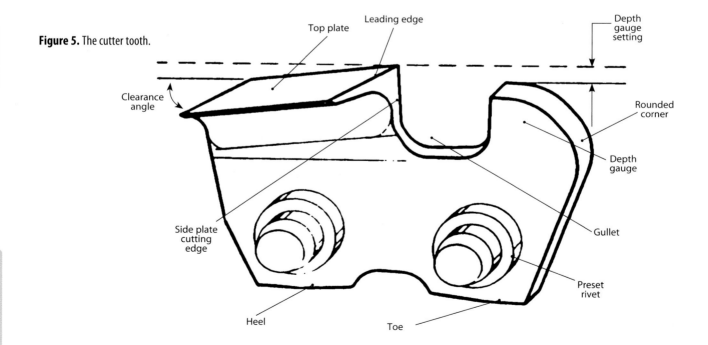

## GUIDE BAR

The guide bar guides the chain so it can do its cutting. Bars are made from one solid piece of hardened steel or constructed of three laminated pieces.

The nose (tip) of the guide bar is the rounded area where the chain reverses direction and returns to the drive sprocket. This tip can be either solid with Stellite (a chromium cobalt alloy) welded on it to reduce wear (bottom in **Figure 6**) or it can have a sprocket in it to further reduce bar tip wear (two center bars in **Figure 6**). Since touching the tip to the wood can be a major cause of kickback, some manufacturers make a special covered tip guard (top bar in **Figure 6**). (For more about kickback, see pages 18–20)

A slot goes all the way around the bar. The drive links of the chain ride in this slot, and therefore the long, thin sides of the slot are subject to wear. (For more about checking wear in the bar, see page 173).

## OIL PUMP

The rivets and links of the chain and guide bar need constant lubrication and that is the job of the oil pump. (For more about bar and chain oil, see pages 58–60.) Nearly all saws today have an automatic lubrication pumping system. On older saws and some smaller saws, oiling is manually activated through a push button or bulb you work with your thumb. If this is true of your saw, you should press the button at least once before each cut and check the oil level often.

No matter which system your saw has, the oil is pumped onto the chain and bar through a slot or hole in the guide bar. It is important to periodically remove the sprocket cover and make sure the slot or hole is clean of debris.

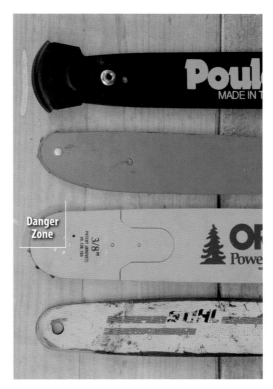

Danger Zone

3/8"

**Figure 6.** The top bar with tip guard is the safest bar you can use, because it prevents the chain from contacting anything in the kickback danger zone. Bars with small-radius tips (second from top) are safer than regular bars, because the kickback zone is smaller. The third bar from the top is a standard, sprocket-nose bar. The bottom bar is a standard bar without a sprocket nose.

## CHAIN BRAKES

Any discussion of how a chainsaw works would not be complete without a mention of the brakes. The best chainsaws have two types of brakes: a manual and an inertial brake.

The front hand guard acts as a manual brake with a hair trigger, not unlike a hand pistol. With even slight pressure on the back of the hand guard, a cocked linkage and powerful spring mechanism goes off and clenches a binder strap on the clutchdrum attached to the chain drive sprocket. The chain is seized almost instantly. It all happens in a matter of milliseconds.

The inertial brake that's built into the front handle/manual brake senses any rotational motion of the saw (such as a kickback) and sets off the cocked linkage that stops the chain automatically. You do not even have to think about doing it yourself. It is like an air bag in a car, just waiting for a chance to prevent an injury (or save a life).

# Glossary

**Anti-Vibration system.** System of either rubber bushings or coil springs located between the engine and the handles used to prevent vibration to the operator's hands (Also called an "anti-vibe" or "AV" system.)

**AWG.** American Wire Gauge. Used to indicate the size of extension cord wires for electric-powered chainsaws. The smaller the gauge number, the thicker the wire in the cord.

**Backcut.** Cut made on the opposite side of the tree from the notched or scarf cut. Also called the "felling cut."

**Bar.** Metal bar that extends from the body of the saw and supports and guides the chain. (Also called the "guide bar.")

**Bar length.** Distance from the cutting tip to where the chain enters the engine housing.

**Bar oil.** Thick, sticky oil used to keep the chain links lubricated as they are cutting. Also called "guide bar oil" and "bar and chain oil." Not to be confused with "two-cycle," "two-stroke," or "premix oil."

**Barber chair.** When a tree splits lengthwise up the trunk while backcutting and ends up looking like a chair. It is usually the result of the tree being windblown or leaning in one direction or being pulled too hard during felling. As the top of the tree falls, it rapidly and unexpectedly springs a slab of tree trunk backwards, opposite the expected line of fall. This is potentially very dangerous.

**Bow saw.** Handsaw with large sharp teeth that is ideal for cutting limbs up to 4 inches in diameter. A safe way to cut spring poles or overhead limbs.

**Brake.** See "inertial brake" and "manual brake."

**Bucking (or to buck).** Process of cutting a felled tree or log into lengths, usually to fit a fireplace or stove.

**Cant hook.** Wooden pole with a pivoting hook and a blunt stub at one end used to roll and move logs.

**Carburetor.** Device in the engine that mixes the fuel and air in the correct proportions, vaporizes them, and sends the mixture to the cylinder.

**Chain.** Loop of riveted-together metal pieces with cutting teeth.

**Chain brake.** A chain brake applies a steel brake band around the driven clutch drum to prevent movement of the saw's cutting chain. The chain brake secures the chain when changing position, moving between cuts or starting a cold saw, and can activate under kickback conditions to prevent the operator being struck by a running chain.

**Chain catcher.** Usually a metal protrusion on the underside of the saw in front of the drive sprocket to prevent a broken or derailed chain from being driven by the drive sprocket.

**Chain gauge.** Thickness of the drive link in the chain. It must fit the groove in the guide bar. Most homeowner saws have a .050" gauge.

**Chaps.** Two pairs of joined leather leggings worn over ordinary trousers to protect the legs. Often made of nylon and/or Kevlar or similar chain-stopping material.

**Chock.** Wedge or block used to secure a log from moving while cutting.

**Choke.** Device that controls the air to fuel ratio that is supplied to the engine.

**Clearance angle.** Slight difference between the rear of the top plate and leading edge on the cutter tooth that makes room for a chip. Without a clearance angle, there would not be a chip and therefore no cut.

**Clutch.** Device that enables two rotating shafts (sprocket and crankshaft) to be connected and disconnected smoothly.

**Cord.** A pile of stacked firewood that is 8 feet long, 4 feet high, and 4 feet deep (128 cubic feet).

**Crown.** Branches and upper weight of a tree. Observing the crown might help determine which direction a tree will fall when cut.

**Cutter.** Part of the chain that contains the cutting edge. Also called "tooth."

**Depth gauge.** Rounded forward edge of each cutter tooth on the chain that prevents the saw from taking too deep of a cut.

**Dogs, bumper spikes, log claw.** Spiked protrusions on one or both sides of the guidebar and attached to the saw body.

**Drive link.** Middle strand of links on a chain whose hook-shaped bottom edges fit into the chain track on the guide bar and engage the teeth on the drive sprocket.

**Drop start.** A very dangerous starting method where only one handle is held and the starter rope is pulled with the other hand. The saw is not immobilized. This starting method is not recommended! (Also called "throw start.")

**Engine displacement.** Total engine volume displaced by the piston. Typically measured in cubic inches (cu. in.) or cubic centimeters (cc). The larger the engine displacement, the more power.

**Entanglement.** Two trees that are entwined or connected by way of a climbing vine. It can be very dangerous to try to fell one of the trees because it is liable to hang up and pivot out of control through the air.

**Escape route.** Safe, pre-determined route of retreat once a tree starts to fall. Clear it of brush and other obstructions.

**Face cord.** A pile of stacked firewood that is 8 feet long, 4 feet high, and 1 to 3 feet deep (Also called a partial cord or a rick.)

**Felling.** Process of cutting down a tree.

**Felling cut.** Cut made on the opposite side of the tree from the notching (scarf) cut. (Also called the "backcut.")

**File guide.** Device that holds and helps position a round file when manually sharpening a chain.

**Flooding the engine.** When too much liquid fuel is in the engine cylinder to allow the engine to start. Excess fuel must evaporate before the engine will be able to start.

**Front hand guard.** Guard in front of the front handle that protects the operator's left hand.

**Fuel stabilizer.** Liquid mixed with the fuel to lengthen the shelf life of gasoline. Unstabilized gasoline has a shelf life of six months or less.

**Gas-to-oil ratio.** The mixture of gasoline to 2-cycle engine oil as measured in volume. It can vary from saw to saw but is generally in the range of 40:1 to 50:1, but some synthetics can be mixed up to 100:1.

**Grubbing.** Digging around a tree stump to pull it out of the ground.

**Guide bar.** Metal bar that extends from the body of the saw and supports and guides the chain. (Also called the "bar.")

**Guide bar gauge.** Width of the groove of a guide bar. Must correspond to chain gouge—usually .050 inch.

**Guide bar nose.** Tip or end of the guide bar. Catching the upper quadrant of the guide bar nose when the chain is in motion will cause kickback.

**Gullet.** Rounded groove in a cutter tooth between the cutting edge and the depth gauge. The gullet carries the new chip out of the cut.

**Hanger.** A tree that gets hung up on another tree(s) as it falls. There can be tremendous stresses and you should not attempt to fell the supporting tree. Hangers can be prevented by carefully planning a clear path for the original tree to fall into.

**Head.** Part of the chainsaw that contains the engine or motor (not the chain or guide bar). (Also called the "saw body" or "power head.")

**Hinge.** When felling a tree, the area left between the notch cut and the felling cut. The trunk will pivot on the hinge causing the tree to fall. The width of the hinge should be approximately ten percent of the diameter of the tree.

**Inertial brake.** Brake that stops the chain upon kickback merely from the rotational motion of the saw.

**Kerf.** Cut made by a saw or the width of a saw cut.

**Kevlar.** Reinforcing material used in chaps to bind the drive sprocket and stop a moving chain to protect from injury.

**Kickback.** Quick backward and upward motion of the guide bar, often towards the operator. Usually occurs when the upper quadrant of the guide bar tip touches an object while the chain is moving.

**Leading edge.** Sharp edge on the chain's cutting tooth.

**Lead-ins.** Funnel-shaped area where the chain enters or exits the guide bar.

**Limbing.** Process of cutting limbs from a felled or standing tree.

**Lopper (also called "lopping shears").** Cutting hand tool that acts like a giant scissors with long handles. Can cut limbs up to 1½ inches in diameter.

**Manual brake.** Connected to a part of the front hand guard. When pushed forward it stops the chain in milliseconds.

**Maul.** Similar to an ax, but with a wider head shaped more like a wedge.

**Milling.** Process of cutting a log into flat lumber or slabs. Usually done with an attachment to the chainsaw's bar.

**Notch cut.** Cut made to create a wedge-shaped notch in a tree that directs the fall of the tree. The wedge faces the desired direction of fall. (Also called a "scarf cut.")

**Oiler control.** System for oiling guide bar and chain. It can be manually operated or automatic.

**Overbuck.** Cutting a log, moving the chainsaw down from the top to the bottom.

**Partial cord.** See face cord.

**Peavy.** A wooden pole with a pivoting hook and a sharp stout point at one end used to roll and move logs.

**Pinch.** Situation where guide bar and chain is stuck within a cut and cannot easily be removed.

**Pitch.** Distance between the centerlines of three adjacent rivets on the chain divided by two. Measured in fractions or thousandths of an inch. This must match the spacing on the

drive sprocket. (Also called "chain pitch.")

**Pole saw.** Small electric or gas-powered chainsaw or manually powered saw mounted on an extension pole that can extend up to 12 feet.

**Poll.** Blunt or broad end of an ax. Often used to drive in wedges.

**Pre-mixed fuel.** Convenient way to buy chainsaw fuel usually sold in a quart-size can. It includes high-octane gasoline, two-cycle engine oil, and a fuel stabilizer.

**Pruning.** Process of cutting limbs from a living tree. (Also called "trimming.")

**Pry pole.** Sturdy sapling or limb that can be used to leverage under a log. Often used to release a pinched guide bar.

**Pull-in.** Force that pulls the saw and operator in toward the wood. It happens when cutting on the bottom of the guide bar.

**Push-back.** Force that pushes the saw and operator away from the wood. It happens when cutting on the top of the guide bar and can lead to kickback.

**Raker.** Front portion of the cutter that contains the depth gauge. Sometimes called the "drag" because it drags or rakes the chips produced by the teeth.

**Rick.** See face cord.

**Rim sprocket.** Type of sprocket that can be interchanged from the clutch drum.

**Safety throttle.** Mechanism that will not allow the trigger to be pulled unless you have a firm grip on the rear handle. Also called "throttle trigger interlock."

**Saw chain gauge.** Thickness of the drive link tangs that fit into the guide bar groove. Measured in thousandths of an inch.

**Sawbuck.** Special sawhorse designed to hold logs in a comfortable and secure position while cutting (bucking) them to length.

**Scabbard.** A housing that slides over the bar and chain when the saw is not in use to prevent damage to the chain or operator.

**Scarf cut.** Cut made to create a wedge-shaped notch in a tree that directs the fall of the tree. The wedge faces the desired direction of fall. (Also called a "notch cut.")

**Scrench.** A tool used for chainsaw maintenance. It consists of a socket mounted to the end of a flat screwdriver.

**Side plate.** Outside face of the cutter tooth.

**Spark arrestor.** Screen across the muffler that keeps sparks from being ejected and thus prevents fires.

**Spring poles.** Small trees (saplings) or branches that are bent over and held down under the weight of a felled tree or limb. These are dangerous, as they can fly back toward you when you cut them or when you cut a limb that is holding them down.

**Sprocket.** Toothed wheel that drives the chain. (Also called the "drive sprocket.")

**Sprocket pitch.** Sprocket size that must correspond with chain pitch.

**Sprocket wheel.** Toothed wheel found in the tip of some chainsaw bars.

**Spur sprocket.** Type of chain drive sprocket that is welded to the clutch drum.

**Starter reel.** Pull rope, handle, and spring assembly used to start the engine. (Also called "recoil starter.")

**Stump vise.** Small vise to securely hold a chainsaw when sharpening the chain in the field.

**Throw bag.** Weighted bag with a line on it used to put a rope in a tree without climbing.

**Tie strap.** Part of the chain that maintains proper spacing between the cutters.

**Timber jack.** Tool used to lift a log off the ground for easier and safer bucking.

**Top plate.** Area on the top of the cutter tooth of the chain. File guide rests on this when sharpening.

**Two-cycle (two-stroke) oil.** Petroleum or synthetic-based oil that is mixed with gasoline to power and lubricate a two-cycle engine such as a chainsaw. (Also called "two-stroke oil" or "premix oil.") Not to be confused with "chain oil" or "bar oil."

**Two-stroke (two-cycle) engine.** Typical engine on a chainsaw. Intake, power, and exhaust occur on the downward stroke of the piston. Compression occurs on the upstroke of the piston. Two-stroke engines provide high power and are light in weight.

**Undercutting (also called "underbucking").** Cutting up from the bottom of a log.

**Wedge.** Tapered piece of metal, plastic, or wood driven into a kerf to open it up. Often used to split wood, prevent the log from pinching the bar and chain, or to help lean the tree toward the intended line of fall. (In this case, they are called "felling wedges" and have a slighter taper than splitting wedges.)

**Widow maker.** Dead branches that can become dislodged and fall unexpectedly when felling a tree. These should be removed by a professional.

**50fuel.com**
Engineered 2-cycle engine fuels for weed eaters, leaf blowers, or chainsaws.

**Amsoil.com**
The original synthetic motor oil.

**ArboristSite.com**
Online forums: "Homeowner Helper," Tree Care, Sponsor, Equipment.

**Baileysonline.com**
Chainsaws, water pumps, generators, safety gear, portable sawmills, and firewood processing equipment.

**Chainsaw.net**
Professional chainsaw sculptors, events, exhibitions, carving chainsaws, and online videos (including author Brian Ruth and other sculptors in action).

**Chainsawbuddy.com**
The Chainsaw Buddy is designed to cut downed wood without grounding the chain, while also "holding" the wood in place.

**GoldEagle.com**
Engine performance and maintenance chemicals.

**Granberg.com**
Chainsaw mills, maintenance/sharpening tools, chain, chain repair tools, "Clip-N-Trim" hedge trimming attachment.

**HaddonTools.com**
Haddon Lumbermaker and Haddon Wood Joiner.

**Hud-Son.com**
Chainsaw mills, tools (hand and power), accessories, measuring tools, splitters, on-line videos.

**Husqvarna.com**
Outdoor power products for forestry, park maintenance and lawn and garden care. Product range includes products for consumers as well as professional users.

**LogSplitters-IronOak.com**
Commercial-grade log splitters and wood handling products.

**Logwizard.com**
Chainsaw attachment that turns that tool into a debarker, planer, jointer, notcher, or post sharpener.

**OregonChain.com**
Saw chain, guide bars, sprockets, and sharpening tools for chainsaws.

**Quickstixmfg.com**
Home of the Quick Stix, a user-friendly device for measuring firewood while it is being cut.

**Rapcoindustries.com**
Carbide chain for use in extremely harsh environments.

**SafeguardVentures.com**
The Centurion™ Chainsaw Guard protects chainsaw operators from kickback and fits most standard size chainsaws.

**APPENDIX**

# More Great Project Books from Fox Chapel Publishing

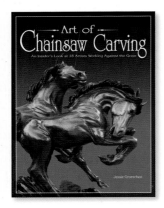

### Art of Chainsaw Carving
*An Insider's Look at 18 Artists Working Against the Grain*
**By Jessie Groeschen**

A profile of leading chainsaw carvers and their work, with a step-by-step project for a chainsaw-carved chair.

ISBN: 978-1-56523-250-1
**$19.95** · 160 Pages

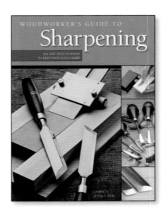

### Woodworker's Guide to Sharpening
*All You Need to Know to Keep Your Tools Sharp*
**By John English**

See the sharpening stations of Sam Maloof, Norm Abram, and other craftsmen as you learn all you need to know about sharpening.

ISBN: 978-1-56523-309-6
**$19.95** · 168 Pages

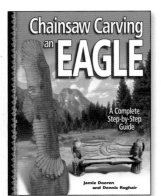

### Chainsaw Carving an Eagle
*A Complete Step-by-Step Guide*
**By Jamie Doeren and Dennis Roghair**

Step-by-step projects for carving an eagle head plaque, a standing eagle with a fish, a soaring eagle, and an eagle bench.

ISBN: 978-1-56523-253-2
**$16.95** · 80 Pages

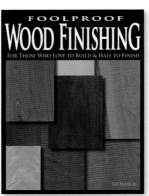

### Foolproof Wood Finishing
*The Complete Guide for Those Who Love to Build and Hate to Finish*
**By Teri Masaschi**

Take the mystery out of finishing and avoid costly mistakes with easy-to-follow exercises designed by woodworking's premier finishing instructor.

ISBN: 978-1-56523-303-4
**$19.95** · 200 Pages

### The New Complete Guide to the Bandsaw
*Everything You Need to Know About the Most Important Saw in the Shop*
**By Mark Duginske**

Everything you need to know to master the workshop's most versatile tool. Contains over 500 photographs and illustrations.

ISBN: 978-1-56523-318-8
**$19.95** · 200 Pages

### New Woodworker Handbook
*The Basics of Spending Wisely, Working Safely & Having Fun in Your Shop*
**By Tom Hintz**

All you need to get started in woodworking is found in this helpful handbook. Includes tips, techniques, tool overviews, shop setup, and detailed woodworking plans.

ISBN: 978-1-56523-297-6
**$19.95** · 264 Pages

In addition to being a leading source of woodworking books and DVDs, Fox Chapel also publishes two premiere magazines. Released quarterly, each delivers premium projects, expert tips and techniques from today's finest woodworking artists, and in-depth information about the latest tools, equipment, & materials.

## Subscribe Today!
*Woodcarving Illustrated:* **888-506-6630**
*Scroll Saw Woodworking & Crafts:* **888-840-8590**
www.FoxChapelPublishing.com